Lessons
in
Living

ANCHOR BOOKS

DOUBLEDAY

New York London

Toronto Sydney

Auckland

Lessons in Living

Susan L. Taylor

⚓

AN ANCHOR BOOK
PUBLISHED BY DOUBLEDAY
a division of Bantam Doubleday Dell Publishing Group, Inc.
1540 Broadway, New York, New York 10036

ANCHOR BOOKS, DOUBLEDAY, and the portrayal of an anchor are
trademarks of Doubleday, a division of Bantam Doubleday Dell
Publishing Group, Inc.

The author gratefully acknowledges permission for the following quotes:
page 155–56 by James W. Rouse; page 160 by Broadside Press; page 138
from *The Prophet* by Kahlil Gibran, copyright 1923 by Kahlil Gibran and renewed 1951 by Administrators C.T.A. of Kahlil Gibran Estate and Mary G.
Gibran, reprinted by permission of Alfred A. Knopf, Inc; opening poem excerpted from *A Dark and Splendid Mass*, published by Harlem River Press,
1992, by permission of the author.

Book design by Terry Karydes
Cover design by LaVon Leak-Wilks

Library of Congress Cataloging-in-Publication Data
Taylor, Susan L.
   Lessons in living / by Susan L. Taylor.
   p.   cm.
   1. Spiritual life.   I. Title.
BL624.T397   1995
291.4'3—dc20   95-8975   CIP

*F*or our ancestors, who live through us and who taught us to obey—and to rebel.

And for Lady T, DorisJean and Phyllis, three rebellious spirits who lived, loved and have being in the hearts of those they touched.

Acknowledgements

I give thanks:

To my sweetie, my husband, Khephra Burns, who is my teacher and my friend. To my daughter, Nequai Taylor, and my sister and brother, Lillian Baker and Larry Taylor, for their love.

To these *Essence* editors: Rosemarie Robotham, for polishing the manuscript and for her love, dedication and encouragement; Derryale Barnes, for critiquing the text and asking the right questions; Charlotte Wiggers, for her expert editing and copyediting; Diane Weathers, for affirming and supporting me; Linda Villarosa and Pamela Johnson, and *Essence* art director Janice Wheeler, whose commitment to the magazine allowed me the freedom to write; and *Essence* associate art director LaVon Leak-Wilks, for the cover design of this book; and to Sherrill Clarke and Janice Bryant, for their painstaking proofreading.

To my editor at Anchor, Roger Scholl; literary agents Marie Brown and Faith Childs; and my coworkers Debra Parker, Angela Kinamore and Regina Barrier for their assistance and care.

And to Eric Butterworth, the wise Unity minister whose Sunday sermons and writings have contributed so much to my happiness.

Contents

I will bring you a whole person
and you will bring me a whole person
and we will have us twice as much
of love and everything . . .

—*excerpted from "Celebration" by Mari Evans*

Introduction

*I*t wasn't the first time I'd stretched myself over the edge, but this time I was terrified. I felt I was losing my grip, losing myself, and I wanted—*needed*—to scream. Not one of those shrill, nerve-rending shrieks, but a wordless primal wail—a cry for help, for mercy, for release from the fears and pressures that had taken hold of my life. For weeks I could feel it rising up inside me, rising from the depths of my soul, even as I fought to contain it.

I was the fashion and beauty editor of *Essence*, and I was

on location in paradise, in the glorious Caribbean, where I had taken a team of photographers, editors and hair and makeup stylists to shoot a cover and fashion layout for the magazine. We had dreamed of this trip for so long, and finally, there we were in magical sun-drenched Jamaica with Iman, at the time the most sought-after model in the world. We wanted to photograph the regal Somalian beauty against a visual feast of bright island flora, white sandy beaches and clear tranquil waters. We wanted to immerse ourselves in the history and the culture of the country, to tap the enduring spirit of the Motherland that had traveled there with our ancestors over the seas and the centuries.

But as the task at hand became clear, I could see that this was not going to be the idyllic trip I had envisioned. The heat was on. We had a week to get all our shots, and the locations we had chosen were scattered throughout the country. Simply getting to each site was a daily logistic challenge that threatened to cause the entire project to unravel in my hands. The crew was large, the tons of equipment and trunks of clothing we'd brought for the shoot were unwieldy, and all of it had to be on the road before dawn each day to catch the best light. Any glitch in executing our plans could cost us time and the magazine money. To complicate matters, it was Iman's first shoot in Ja-

maica and the press followed us everywhere, clamoring to photograph and interview her.

Both Iman and I had brought our children along—little Zuleka, Iman's rambunctious two-year-old daughter, and my own precocious Shana-Nequai, who was ten. The responsibility for making the shooting a success was mine, and each day I felt the pressure steadily mounting. Looking back now, I wonder if Nequai's determined helpfulness on the trip was born of an instinctive understanding of my fragile emotional state.

I can see it so clearly. For years I'd been racing through each day, not living my life, not owning it. I was driven, trying to cover all the bases at home and at work while wrestling inwardly with insecurity. For some time I'd been going round and round in tighter and tighter circles, arriving again and again at the same wordless pain. The people, places and predicaments changed, but the emotional landscape was always the same—stress, doubt and fear.

Until then I'd always managed to move through my inner turmoil. But on those winding roads that took us through the lush green hills of Jamaica, my anxieties were spinning out of control. I'd held everything in, maintained my composure for so long. Now I was losing it.

Like my mother, Babs, I'm prone to depression. Even as a child I felt an inexplicable sadness and isolation. I longed

to be loved and cherished. I often felt as though I'd been born into the wrong family, a chatty lovebug trapped in a house with quiet people who never touched. I was still a little girl when I began to search wildly for affection. I would run to my grandmother's embrace, to my girlfriends' homes, to the groping hands of boys in my Harlem neighborhood. Throughout my teens and well into adulthood, I searched for ways to ease the anxiety that was always within me. I looked everywhere, and at times in dangerous places.

At twenty I ran to marriage. I hooked up with Billy for all the wrong reasons: He was so handsome; he was crazy about me; he made lots of money in his thriving beauty salon. Billy was ten years my senior, and in some ways he helped satisfy the hunger I felt for my father's affection. But by the third summer of our marriage, I was pregnant and living in our beautifully furnished Bronx apartment, depressed and alone. Billy was having an affair with a woman who worked for him, and he'd stopped coming home.

Suddenly my security was gone. I felt defenseless, abandoned and humiliated. I didn't want my family to know how miserable I was throughout my pregnancy, though at times I thought I'd never stop crying. Even today my breath catches in my chest when I think about how much I hurt that summer.

Still, I stayed. Nequai was born, and when she was six

weeks old, after an explosive confrontation with Billy, I left the marriage. I was on the run again, trying to fill what now felt like a gaping hole within me. I did everything to escape from the pain. I ran to my mother. And I ran away from her. I ran to religion. I ran to a new relationship, then back to my marriage and out of it again.

I tumbled out of wedlock into single-motherhood, facing one financial crisis after another. In 1970 I landed a part-time freelance position as beauty editor at the new magazine *Essence*. By 1972 I'd been promoted to the high-profile job of fashion and beauty editor, but the publication was in financial crisis, and all the young staff members' salaries were low.

I was struggling on every front. Struggling to pay my bills. Struggling to hold on to my apartment. Struggling to be a good mother when at times I didn't want to be there. Struggling to be a good daughter to my own mother, who never learned to bridle her tongue, who always said what she felt and never bothered to soften her words to spare my feelings. And there was pressure on the job—disapproving eyes on me as I'd ease out of late meetings and rush to pick up my daughter from day care. I was responsible for creating the *Essence* covers and the fashion and beauty pages, and sometimes I'd have to reshoot stories until the senior editors felt I had gotten them right. I was always in some photographer's studio. And when photo sessions ran late, one of the editors who worked with me would dash out and pick up Nequai, and we'd keep her with us in those chilly loft spaces until late into the night.

Fear and insecurity were constantly eating away at me. Unlike all the people I worked with—even those who reported to me—I hadn't gone to college. Unlike the other editors, I didn't have a literary background. My entree to *Essence* was as a 24-year-old high-school graduate who had created a successful line of beauty products. I was a cosmetologist, not a journalist. And truth be told, in the early days of the magazine I didn't even know what a fashion and beauty editor was supposed to do! Yet I had to manage a staff, direct the studio sessions, generate images and write or supervise copy without having a clue about how to do any of those things.

I was in over my head. I was overwhelmed by the responsibilities that were taking over my life, stressed out from parenting solo and from the effort of faking it much of the time. A litany of fears haunted me. I was afraid that all the smart, accomplished people in my world would discover that I was a fraud. Afraid that I'd never earn enough to stop worrying about money. Afraid that I'd blown my chance for a stable life by marrying young and becoming a mother be-

fore I was emotionally or financially ready. I was afraid that I'd never find a satisfying love relationship.

With my many fears tenuously contained, I greeted the world each day buffed and polished like the models I presented on the pages of the magazine. My clothing, hair, nails and makeup—all impeccably done, and no one seemed to notice the cracks lengthening beneath the facade of cheerfulness I wore like armor. I became so skilled at the masquerade that even I began to believe it was real.

I'm not sure I could have articulated back then what I was feeling or fleeing, but during that pressured photo shoot in Jamaica I knew it was all catching up with me. The feelings of inadequacy that had plagued me for most of my life were overtaking me. The mask of competence and confidence was becoming transparent.

In Jamaica I could feel myself withdrawing, wanting to be alone, to be away from the team and the children buzzing around me. I could barely look anyone in the eye. I was fighting to keep my cool, my hands steady and my knees strong. I was tired, so tired. Tired of directing, tired of having to answer questions, tired of being Mommy, tired of being the responsible daughter, tired of juggling. Tired of holding in the scream.

There in Jamaica, on an afternoon when the blinding

midday sun had chased our shadows underfoot and the team indoors for lunch, I found my moment. I walked alone to the end of a wooden pier that reached into the cleansing blue waters. There, with only the splash of waves before me, it came. With my arms flung wide and my head thrown back, it came again and again—a scream that unfurled from the core of my being, carrying my fears, my tears and my frustrations into the wind. I asked God for mercy. Then, to order and direct my life. The moment I surrendered, peace embraced me. My healing had begun.

Some time after we had returned to New York City, I was working late one night with Sandra Martin, then our associate fashion and beauty editor. Sandra is an open and honest person, a beautiful sister, and she always watched my back. That evening we were discussing the photo shoot in Jamaica—what had gone well, what we might have done differently—when Sandra's eyes softened and she said, ever so gently, "I saw you that afternoon at the beach. I heard you shouting out over the water."

The masquerade was over. There in Jamaica, many miles from home, at the end of a pier that I'd thought was safe harbor, the bright island sun had exposed my pain, and the trade winds sweeping over the Caribbean had carried my cry back to shore.

The compassion and love I'd sought throughout my

life—and that Sandra offered that night—I had never given myself. All my energy had been spent outside of me—on work, family and friends, on love relationships. I had left no space in my life for me. No time for rest and renewal. No time for relaxation and fun. No opportunities for reknitting and rekindling my spirit. Over the years I had learned how to *do*, but not how to *be*. There had been signs all around me—obvious ones that I chose to ignore—that I needed to start loving and nurturing myself. Warnings would come like a tap on the shoulder and then, when I failed to heed them, a slap upside the head. But it would take a knock-down blow for me to see the light.

No matter what we may think or feel, regardless of appearances, life is always on our side, always offering us the experiences we need to make changes and grow. Feeling myself losing myself rerouted me. It prompted me to pursue balance as a goal in my life. And Sandra's nonjudgmental witness to my secret anguish helped untie my tongue. It helped me realize that our silence doesn't protect us or make us less afraid. Keeping our fears secret only gives them more power.

We've all had to face crises in our lives. They are an unavoidable part of our journey. Some cause wrenching pain: A beloved parent dies. A relationship you thought you'd grow old in is gone. A job you planned to retire from

ends. A child you did your best for hurts your heart. No matter who you are, no matter what color or gender you are, how wealthy or educated you are, or how fully you know God, at times the world will bend you and bow you and pitch you off center. But our problems also coax us to look within ourselves, to think more deeply about who we are and about the meaning of our lives.

Our numbing doubts, anxieties, turmoil, despair—all the emotions that at times take hold of us—are rooted in the only problem we really ever have: fear. This fear—the sum total of our negative thinking—surrounds the planet like a thick gray cloud. It touches all of our lives and crowds out our joy. The evidence of fear is everywhere, fueling racism, sexism, violence and greed. Fear blurs our vision, blinds us to truth. It makes us underrate ourselves and our ability to handle the challenges that are a natural and important part of living. Our fears can immobilize us, make us feel alone and unprotected, lost and confused, unable to see the many trails leading out of the woods.

And there is always a way out. The way out is within. There is a sacred place within us where wisdom and clarity dwell. This is where God resides and has being. This is the simple truth we were born to discover. Awakened to this truth, we won't fear the darkness of the night.

We journey for a purpose: to discover our divinity and

to use its power. Life is work, and we are created with all the tools to attend to the many tasks along our journey. At the end of our lives, this world should be a better place because we have lived here, because we have used our time on earth to become better human beings.

The essays in *Lessons in Living* explore more fully, more deeply what I write about each month in my editorial column in *Essence*, what I wrote about in my first book, *In the Spirit*, and what I'm trying to awaken within myself: faith in our inner wisdom to sustain us despite the trials and traumas in our lives.

Through my work as editor-in-chief of the magazine and my extensive travel over the years, I've become acutely aware that most of us are seeking the same thing: inner peace. So many of the people I meet express a deep hunger for a practical spirituality that offers sustenance and meaning in their daily lives. Those feelings and that need are also my own.

Lessons in Living explores the importance of loving and honoring ourselves, which is an ongoing challenge for me. The principles shared here are those I'm trying to live by because, despite my unending challenges, despite my losses and fears, they help me stay connected to my inner resources of power and wisdom and maintain balance and peace in my life.

Lessons in Living demonstrates, through the challenges I have faced in my life and those encountered by others, that the human spirit is irrepressible, and that problems can be a source of pain or of empowerment, depending on the value and meaning we give them.

I wrote *Lessons in Living* because our children are in crisis, and we are their only hope. But in order to secure them and the many among us who are floundering, we must find security within ourselves. We must have faith in our innate goodness and wholeness and the unlimited power we possess to attain inner peace. By cultivating a personal relationship with God and living reflectively, we can break negative, destructive patterns and open the way to love, health and happiness in our lives. As wisdom and faith emerge from within us, we recognize that we are always in God's embrace. In *Lessons in Living* I've tried to offer practical and simple ways for us to live that truth so that we may achieve what we are seeking most: inner peace and joy. Until we allow peace and joy to unfold from within us, we will forever be distracted from doing our larger critical work. Only when we expand the promise of our lives will we have the courage, the vision and the will to provide a lifeline to those who are suffering still.

The Purpose of the Journey

There is so much to learn during the journey of a lifetime, so many lessons in living to absorb along the way. There are lessons in loving, in developing patience, in cultivating tolerance, in practicing humility, courage and faith. Lessons in doing and being. All this unsought instruction and guidance is meant to point us to the one truth we are born to discover: that we are more than we seem. That there is an aspect of our being that is invulnerable and immortal. God lives within us; we are human and divine.

No matter where we are on our life's journey, no matter what our circumstances are, we can draw from each and every experience some wisdom that helps us grow in awareness of our divinity. Imagine the freedom from anxiety, the inner peace we would feel if we truly believed that we are guided and protected by the love within. Imagine the enthusiasm with which we would examine our lives if we knew that hidden in the challenges we all face are blessings tailor-made to benefit us. Seeking wisdom would be our most important task. Our lives would become less of a struggle as we put up less resistance to the painful but positive changes Spirit is leading us through. Knowing that, regardless of appearances, a divine order is always at work, we would develop the patience of wise souls who placidly ride out life's storms knowing that these, too, shall pass. We would no longer be held captive by the tyranny of our own ungoverned emotions. We would be free.

With such a larger view of existence, we would see ourselves as we are—as spiritual beings created to become channels for the love that created us, for the power we call God. But most people live and die without discovering that fundamental truth about themselves. We come to adulthood believing our eyes are open to the ways of the world, when in fact we must devote a lifetime to our awakening. The creative spirit of God lives in us, and it is greater than our pain

God lives within you; you are human and divine.

or disillusionment or despair. The degree to which we accept and live this truth is the degree to which we stop doing battle with life and are able to look upon its unending challenges with confidence and grace. As we grow in awareness of our divinity, we instinctively turn inward during any crisis to ask what is always the most important question: *What are the lessons that I am to learn from this challenge?*

But who of us comes of age in tune with our innate power or with a ready understanding of what it means to be emotionally mature? Although we are witness to our parents' many trials, few of us grow up anticipating crises of our own. We all feel that somehow we are the exception—that life will provide, that obstacles will be removed or overcome and that any problems that arise will resolve themselves. As children, most of us were protected, spared the burden of responsibility for our lives. Like so many, I came to adulthood expecting mine to be a breeze. I thought I'd graduate from high school, begin my career, move into my own apartment, get married, have children and have a wonderful life. Not once did I consider that tremendous challenges and upsets might also lie ahead. So during the first real crisis of my adult life, when I was in my early twenties and pregnant and my three-year marriage began careening to its bruising end, I was shaken to the core. Fear made retreating seem like an easier option than confronting my pain and taking responsibility for ending it. Losing my man and my emotional and financial security while I was pregnant and unemployed was so emotionally crushing I thought I'd never recover.

At some time in our lives we have all experienced the kind of anxiety that makes us feel as if our world is coming to an end. But in retrospect we can always see that things have a way of working out. Looking back on the crises that were the causes of our mental and emotional anguish, we see from the vantage of hindsight they were not so much an end as a turning point in our lives. I recognize now that the self-doubt, the breaking down and giving up in my own life forced me to take charge of myself and begin building a new emotional home. The challenges made me reach deeper, try harder, grow stronger. I discovered that the only relief from the pain I was feeling lay in surrendering myself to God, in trusting that there is a divine order and master plan at work in the universe. That trust has been justified hundreds of times over the course of the years since then. Now, most days I feel confident and strong. My fears are being replaced with faith, my despair with hope, my sadness with joy—and not in spite of the devastating experiences, but because of them.

When my marriage ended, I was thrown onto my own

resources. I'm sure that if my family had had money, I would have asked them to support me, or at least to pay my rent. But if they had I might have settled for living like a victim and never have gotten out of bed. To my surprise, I found I could stand firm on my own two feet. Single-motherhood anointed me, oriented me, made me stronger. It forced me to grow up and take responsibility for myself.

At times I felt trapped parenting solo. I was young, I wanted to have fun, be free. Now I know that having to care for my daughter, Shana-Nequai, helped save my life. I had to be awake, alert and careful. I couldn't hang out; I had to come home. I had to restrain my appetites. I couldn't invite every man I felt attracted to into my heart or my home. While at times I was reckless, I couldn't allow myself to get swept away by the undertow of those wild times—the wanderlust, free love and recreational drugs that were so much a part of the seventies.

Single-motherhood made me more discerning than I was inclined to be. Being the sole support of my daughter compelled me to think critically about my future, and I began to make plans for us.

God makes no mistakes. In all our trials and dramas there are lessons. Life is not a playground but a classroom, and our journey through life provides us with the course

work and the tests required for our education and development. It offers us the lessons we need to refine ourselves, to realize our profound and often hidden potential. Everything we experience along the path is meant to teach us to respect our divinity, to cooperate with God, and to use the gift of free will to shape and reshape the best life possible. It is through both our triumphs *and* our challenges that God leads us to discover the source of love and use its unlimited reserves to unleash the creativity and strength we possess. Life is the unending process of discovering our great capacity to love, of recognizing that we are human and divine, fully equipped but uninstructed. Life is our finishing school.

The unhappiness we experience is not so much a result of the difficulties encountered along our journey as it is of our misperception of how life instructs us. We may see a failed relationship as an indictment of our self-worth when it is really a lesson in using better judgment, in valuing ourselves more, in expressing greater appreciation for our partner—lessons to prepare us for a more loving and fulfilling union. If we are passed over for a much-anticipated promotion, it may be just the push we need to get more training or to venture out on our own as an entrepreneur. As we rise to meet the challenges that are a natural part of living, we

The lessons along your path are God's invitation to you to grow.

awaken to our many undiscovered gifts, to our inner power and our purpose.

Although we may be unaware of it, God is always urging us forward, giving us the experiences we need to surrender the mistaken ideas, bad habits and unhealthy relationships that burden us. There are no meaningless experiences: Every interaction, every event along our journey has significance, because it shapes how we perceive ourselves and how we view life. We can find hidden truth in each situation by holding it up to our own divine light. Rather than simply responding emotionally to a challenge, we must practice looking within ourselves to discover the meaning of our experiences. The key is our ability to pause—to put aside our egos and suspend judgment long enough to allow that still, small voice within to be heard. Once we make that mental shift, we can begin to view our lives from a higher perspective. The truth is that everything—a lover's betrayal, a parent's harsh remark, even a health challenge—is a lesson for our growth, not for our oppression. Our lives become a painful journey only when we resist, rather than accept, the lessons on our path that are God's invitation to grow.

I think back to the loneliness I felt after the breakup of my first marriage, and how I hungered for a love relation-

ship. But it was that loneliness that led me to books on spirituality, and solitude that allowed me to pursue them at length. With the inspiration and guidance I found in those books I was able to create more happiness than I had known in the best days of my marriage. So much of who I am today is a result of that experience.

If your life were everything you wished it to be, what would your purpose be? What would you be doing here? What would encourage you to extend yourself, to be inventive and grow into the fullness of your being? There'd be little development or activity in your life. As long as we are alive we are in the process of becoming. Our birth is an unending act; there is always more growing to do. Holding fast to that awareness reduces our resistance to life's challenges and helps us to meet them creatively.

Years after that marriage ended, I saw what, in retrospect, was probably evident all the while: The path I'd been following wasn't the right one for me. I hadn't questioned my direction or realized that what I was settling for was superficial satisfaction. I had chosen what was attractive and what I'd been taught was safe, but not what was true for me. Though there are undoubtedly those who know early and instinctively what their mission is and pursue it with a single-minded purpose, life may have to lead others of us with not-so-subtle hints, even knock us down a few times before

we finally look up and observe the signposts pointing toward our greater happiness. Even when we are unconscious of it, God is encouraging us to keep striving, to expand the promise of our lives, to fulfill the purpose of our journey.

Challenges are as fundamental to our existence as air. Struggle strengthens. Without the threat of predators and the challenge of the hunt, our primate ancestors would not have developed their haunches and stood upright to peer above the tall grasses of the African savanna. Standing upright freed their hands for grasping, tearing, manipulating and toolmaking. This then freed their mouths for speech, which in turn hastened the evolution of intelligent human brains.

We continue to evolve as a species—and individually. The difficulty of moving heavy objects from place to place inspired the invention of the wheel. We owe our very dreams of flight, of soul-soaring freedom, to the gravity that keeps us earthbound. Without the physical challenges of managing our environment, our muscles would atrophy, our bones grow brittle. Without life's inevitable challenges to our survival, our freedom, our happiness, we might never discover our resourcefulness. We might never search within ourselves for wisdom, strength or truth. We might never seek God.

Each of us is a unique and divine original, created on

purpose, with a purpose. We didn't just happen. We were billions of years in the making, refined and perfected throughout eons of evolution. Consider the ordeals our ancestors had to survive in order for us to be. We are here because they didn't give up. The wisdom and grace and sheer determination of their response to adversity should both inspire and reassure us. They came through much tougher times than we will ever know. Even in the face of holocaust and genocide, they refused to succumb to despair, refused to die. They survived because they took strength and direction from their intimate, trusting relationship with God.

Although they struggled fiercely, the generations before us who paved our way were bolstered by their certainty about life. As a child I would stop playing hopscotch or jumping double Dutch to listen to the hopeful voices that rose from the little storefront church in my Harlem neighborhood: "I'm so glad trouble don't last always," the elders would sing. They understood that day always follows night. In their darkest hours they kept moving forward, knowing that God was leading them even when *they* couldn't see the light. We are the children of those stalwart women and men. Their blood flows through our veins, and the wisdom, tenacity and faith that secured them are our inheritance.

God has prepared us for this hour by giving birth to us

over time. In order for us to be, countless stars had to be born and die, and in death give birth to others, to our sun, the planets and life. We are part of this divine order, part of God's perfect plan. Science tells us we are literally made of star stuff, of radiant energy and light. We possess the same transformative power for creating worlds.

We need not look to the heavens or anywhere outside ourselves for a miracle to transform our lives. *Life* is the miracle. *You* are the miracle, for you are made in the image and likeness of God. In our minds we have made God human, but in fact it is *we* who are divine. God is not like us; but we are Godlike, because we, too, have the power to create the lives and the world we want. We are partners with God, cocreators. We are the hands of God, migrant workers sent to earth with all the talents and strengths needed to do God's work—here for a season to explore a world of possibilities for personal growth and for making the world a better place.

Life is a journey, forever unfolding. This is one of the essential truths in the biblical and historical accounts of Jesus and his disciples. "Come, follow me," Jesus bade them, but never did he say where they were going. The object of their journey lay not in their arrival at a particular destination, but rather in their encounters along the way—in enjoying a wedding feast, in fighting political oppression, in feeding the hungry, healing the sick, surviving a storm at sea.

We deify Jesus, forgetting that he was a man, our brother sent to teach us that the Divine Presence dwells within each of us, longing to express itself through us. "I am the Way, the Truth and the Life. . . . I am in the Father and the Father in me," Jesus taught. Eric Butterworth, the beloved Unity minister, says it this way: "We are the very *self-livingness* of God." Each of us has this divine potential, the Christ potential, the potential that Jesus realized.

We must recognize the divinity within for ourselves: *I am the Way*. That way is the way of the cross—the cross between spirit and matter, between the human and the divine. As we take up the cross, as we embark on our journey, God wants us to realize that while we are heirs to the vulnerability of the flesh, we are also the inheritors of the healing power of the spirit.

Among the desert mystics of North Africa, the Way— "Il-Rah"—is also "the way of the road." It is an apt symbol, for the people of the desert are nomads, and whatever they encounter along their journeys they accept as the lessons that teach them about life. The hajj, the sacred pilgrimage to Mecca, is likewise symbolic of life's journey, with all its hardships and rewards.

Each of us is on a journey. And it is the *way*—the *manner*—in which we respond to the many signposts along the road that determines whether our lives become an adventure or a frustration, a blessing or a burden. The ultimate purpose of our journey, the spiritual treasure that we seek, is enlightenment.

On a spiritual level, we chose to be here at this time and place because we have lessons to learn and contributions to make. We are here to transform ourselves and, in so doing, transform the world.

At times along the way we stumble, we stub our toes, we scrape our knees. We may say or do things that hurt ourselves or others. A selfish act or careless remark may injure a lover or friend. And so we pause to examine the wound, apply the salve and journey on. As we learn the lessons of our journey and carry them forward with us, we become more agile, our feet more sure. We not only avoid the pitfalls, but the very path also gets easier. Even when it takes us over steep, rugged terrain, we must recognize that this, too, is a part of life's landscape. We must remember that such terrain is fleeting, that the scenery will eventually change. The rocks and ridges along the difficult parts of the path are strengthening us and preparing us for whatever lies ahead. And so each day of our journey we should affirm for ourselves: *Whatever I find along my path, I will ask God how to use.*

As we encounter obstacles, let them inspire our creativity. If we lose a valued possession, let us recognize that God is clearing a space in our lives for something of greater value or, more important, reminding us to keep material things in their proper perspective so that we don't lose sight of our purpose in life: to embrace our divinity and learn to love.

Practicing the Presence

Remember when you thought that in order to be happy you had to have that particular home or job or love relationship you wanted so desperately? Remember when you pinned all your hopes on the success of a certain project? Remember when you felt that if the crisis you were facing didn't have the outcome you wanted, you'd never breathe easy again? And how miserable you were when things didn't work out the way you had planned? But remember, after a time, how grateful you were that God had a better plan than yours?

Imagine the anguish you'd avoid if you didn't give way to doubt and fear, but simply did your best and trusted God to take care of the details. Imagine how peaceful you would feel if you believed that no matter what the future has in store, life is always leading you toward your highest good. Imagine how your anxieties and self-doubt would evaporate, and how bravely, how boldly, you'd face the world each day if you understood that now and forever you are loved and protected, always in God's care.

We are born trusting life to care for us, but over time we learn to fear living as much as we fear dying. Pause for a moment and reflect on the concept of God you were taught in your early religious training, learned from your parents, or simply absorbed from the culture. What was your image of God? How did you see yourself in relationship to God? Although religious rituals have evolved greatly since the days of the Old Testament, when burnt offerings of human and animal flesh were meant to pacify an angry and vengeful deity, pleading to God and begging for mercy remain a central part of most Western religions today. Most of us grew up with the concept of a stern God who encouraged our supplication, our bowing down and offering up. We learned to utter rote prayers and praises to a God who lived in the sanctuary or high above the clouds. The God of our traditions was to be feared and appeased. Like that of so many of us, this was my childhood indoctrination.

The nuns who were my elementary-school teachers instilled obedience and discipline, but they also taught that only those who conform to a very narrow and rigid doctrine are worthy of grace and salvation. As a little girl, I remember being afraid that my father would burn in hell. He wasn't Catholic, he didn't go to church every Sunday, and when he did go to worship, it was to the Methodist church —all mortal sins that, according to canon law, damned his soul for all eternity.

I learned to fear God. Just entering the sanctuary made me nervous. I can still see us little East Harlem Catholic schoolgirls—African-American and Caribbean, Puerto Rican, Irish and Italian—all in our blue-and-white uniforms with little beanies on our heads. We'd line up according to size, our heads bowed reverently, palms pressed for prayer as we filed quietly into St. Paul's. We dared not speak or look across the aisle where the boys were getting settled. We moved directly to our pews, genuflected and made the sign of the cross before kneeling for what seemed like hours to recite the rosary. If we dared to doze or rest our behinds on the edge of the pew, taking the pressure off our aching knees, Sister would be on our backs.

But I did love the aroma of frankincense and the purity of the plainsong choir melodies that filled the air. The songs were a meditation for me. Any spiritual experience I had in church as a child was sparked by the music—the soothing Gregorian chants, the moving Christmas hymns and triumphant Easter songs that still touch me deeply. Everything else seemed remote and mysterious. At that time the liturgy was in Latin, so who knew what the priest was saying? I never did learn exactly when to sit, stand or kneel. And even when a few schoolmates and I were the only ones in the church, we were afraid to speak above a whisper. I never felt easy in the sanctuary. I was always fearful I'd break something precious—a statue of a saint, the vase with flowers at the Blessed Mother's feet, a glass holding a votive candle.

But it was weekly confession that made me most anxious. I would enter the small, dark booth ready to lie. There was no way I was telling Father McSherry any of the "sins" I'd committed since my last "confession." Father knew my family, and if my stern West Indian parents ever got wind of my real doings, they would never be as forgiving as God and Father McSherry. So I'd make up little things that I knew he'd quickly absolve me of, giving me a few prayers to say as penance. But then I'd spend the rest of the day feeling guilty and begging God not to condemn my soul.

My friends Barbara and Diane were Pentecostal, and in

their church you were encouraged to make a public confession, to testify in front of the entire congregation as a prelude to being saved. But you weren't truly saved, they'd say, until you were possessed by the Holy Spirit and could speak in tongues. They used to tell me about a particular group of women in their church who every Sunday would try to out-shout one another when the Holy Spirit came down from heaven to take possession of them. Paulette was Baptist, and she had to go to church three times on Sunday—to Sunday school early in the morning, to the eleven o'clock service and to evening prayers—if she wanted to be ready when God came down from heaven to separate the wheat from the chaff. The wheat was the souls of the righteous who would be taken up into heaven, and the chaff, those who didn't go to church, would be thrown into the fire.

All of us grew up trying to reach out and up to a distant God for deliverance. But it was as a young mother in crisis—emerging from a painful marriage, in a job that didn't pay enough for me to meet my expenses, racked with anxiety that had become a physical pain in my chest, and unsure that I had the strength to hold on—that my heart opened to the wisdom shared in a minister's Sunday evening sermon: *God is alive in you,* he repeated, *God is alive in you.* The moment I began to surrender to the simple truth of the Reverend Alfred Miller's words, my suffering began to ease.

While I was focused on my pain I could see no solutions to my problems. But once I changed my attitude about my condition, I saw I had so much I simply took for granted, and room in my life for more than I had ever imagined. With a change in mind and behavior came a change in my circumstances: I was promoted at the magazine, my salary doubled, and new, fulfilling relationships came into my life. As the truth continues to unfold in me today, my fears are replaced with faith.

God doesn't dwell on some distant cloud. God doesn't live in the church or in the temple or within the crystals, crosses and statues that we imbue with attributes of the divine. And God doesn't need our pleas or even our praise. To prostrate ourselves and plead for the things we want doesn't draw them nearer to us. Beseeching a faraway God only engenders feelings of separation and alienation. It is practicing the absence, not the presence, of God.

God is right here, wherever *you* are. God is within you and everywhere around you. God is omnipresent and omniscient. You never have to beg or bargain with God for anything. The Holy Spirit knows your needs even before you do. And it is God's very nature to fulfill your needs, at the time and in the manner that is best for you. There are many lessons we must learn in our lifetime, but none is more essential to our happiness than this one.

God is the love that is breathing for you, the love that is beating your heart.

We never have to entreat God to be more kind or benevolent. God *is* kindness and benevolence. The very substance of God is love—the love that created you and me and all living things. It is the love within the little acorn that becomes the great oak tree, the love that protects the lilies of the field. God is the love that is breathing for you, the love that is beating your heart.

Often it's our childhood indoctrination that is the most difficult to change. But anything that is learned can be unlearned over time. We must begin to unlearn the myth that we are separate from God. God isn't in the clouds, God *is* the clouds. God is the sun and the moon, the grass and the trees, the earth and the sky and everything in between. *God is.*

The walls of fear and separation begin to crumble as you begin to accept what spiritual leader Olga Butterworth teaches, that "God and you *is* one." As you begin to practice the presence of God in you, you establish inner serenity and balance because you feel at one with the heart of life.

Our mind is a powerful and important tool. Our thoughts become things. Mind is the source of all that human beings have created. And it can heal us, emotionally and physically. Even if this is a challenging time in your life, the moment you focus on the divinity within you, you'll feel comforted. Take a few deep breaths. As you think about the

meaning of the truth *God is alive in me; God is alive* as *me*, whisper it to yourself, and you will sense the Presence within you. You won't be able to keep the smile from your lips. You may even laugh out loud with pure joy.

The Great Spirit that brought you forth has never left you. It never will. You may leave God, but the door is always open, awaiting your return. No matter how far you wander or how lost you feel, your anxiety and fear will be washed away by the power that receives you when you surrender your heart to God. You needn't move a muscle. Just turn your attention inward. God knows what *you* want. Once you begin listening inwardly, you'll discover what God wants for you. You'll know which steps to take, which moves to make. Your problems will seem to unravel.

Perhaps you need to leave behind someone or something that undermines your integrity—a relationship that doesn't honor you, a job that doesn't value what you have to offer. When you trust that you are in God's care, you won't fear change, you'll welcome it. Negative thoughts, addictions and egocentric behavior begin to wither because you no longer need them to prop yourself up from the outside. You'll know that God lives within you and is in charge of your life. And your ear will be trained inward—on that still, small voice that is always guiding you, always whispering to you: *All is well.*

We mustn't reserve communing with God just for morning and evening prayers, or for weekly worship service, or for when we feel burdened. The goal is to realize that every moment of our lives is a meditation. Allow yourself to marvel at the wonder of God's work all around us. Throughout your day, let the sun, a tree, a piece of fruit remind you that everything you could ever want has been provided and can be found right here on earth. While changing the baby's diaper, give thanks for the miracle of creation you hold in your hands. Contemplate the mind-boggling technologies we have access to today and realize that they are the products of something much greater, of human minds just like yours, and that those minds, like yours, are manifestations of the One Mind, God. The moment you begin to consider God first in everything you do, the world around you softens and your life becomes easier. You'll feel healthier, happier and at peace with yourself.

Maintaining the awareness that God lives within us is a mental exercise. And as with physical exercise, the more we do it, the better we feel. Before you get out of bed to greet the day, take a moment to greet the divinity within you. Lie still, close your eyes and smile toward the indwelling spirit. Give thanks for your life. Then ask God what you should know about your life and this day. And listen. Keep paper and a pen next to your bed so that you can write down your insights. Affirm for yourself that, regardless of circumstances, you are going to remain positive, calm and open to the wisdom of the spirit throughout the day.

Remember, there is no separation between you and God. When you brush your teeth and shower, know that your hands are a manifestation of God. And when you speak and move throughout the day, remember that it is God speaking through you and moving as you. Practicing the presence of God in you fortifies your spirit. It helps you keep negativity at bay so that you begin to experience the rapture and joy of living. And you'll want more and more of it.

This is the spiritual armor I try to don each day when I immerse myself in the healing waters of a warm bath and am reminded of the divine love that surrounds and protects me wherever I am; when I walk and allow the simple rhythm of putting one foot in front of the other to become a mantra for my meditations. I've learned that by fortifying myself from within throughout the day, the anxieties I would regularly have about meeting my many deadlines, about family matters and relationships, dissolve and make room for me to look for solutions that always unfold in divine order.

When you pray, remember that you are not praying to a distant God, but to the God that dwells within you. Don't just speak the words; feel what they mean in your life. Don't

The more you are aware of God's unchanging love, the safer you feel in the world.

pray from your lips, but from your heart. Your prayers aren't for God, they are for you, to remind you of the presence of the Holy Spirit within you. When you say "Thy kingdom come, thy will be done," remember that you are loved and protected. God has planned greater things for us than we can imagine. The more we maintain an awareness of God's unchanging love, the safer and more at home we will feel in the world.

Each one of us has a finite amount of time on earth, but it's enough time to do the work that only we can do, the work we were sent here to do. Don't waste a moment of your precious life worrying. Worry is counter to the flow of life. It is a lone and ineffectual *no* drowned out by the over-whelming *yes* that is life. It clouds the vision and taxes our health and vitality. Remember to put God first in everything you do. Lay your plans, move your feet and trust Spirit to do the rest. Never forget that God's protective love is al-ways sheltering you. The indwelling spirit is forever guiding you. As your awareness of God's presence in your life ex-pands, you will feel a peace that surpasses all understand-ing—no matter what unfolds.

37

*B*ecause I write and speak about the transforming power of the spirit within us, some folks assume that I have it all together and my life is rarely a struggle. The question I'm asked most often during my travels is how I always manage to remain hopeful and calm. Many people are surprised when I tell them that I don't—that I, too, get the blues; that sometimes my fears and insecurities lie just beneath the surface of my composure, threatening to upset my balance. And at times they do. But years ago I made up my mind that I wasn't going to linger in a painful place, or choose to live my life in therapy. And I found that I wouldn't have to if I kept my commitment to listen to my inner voice in silence each day.

I talk a lot about the importance of loving ourselves by honoring our needs. I write about it, speak about it, and I know in the depths of my being how important those quiet moments of reflection are to staying connected with our resources of understanding, courage and strength. Yet sometimes, when the world presses closely around me, I abandon the very thing I need most. Often my quiet time, my private time, is the first thing to go. And each time I relinquish my space for rest and renewal, the reins on my life begin to slip from my hands. But I am comforted knowing I can take charge of my life again at any time I choose. How blessed we are that everything needed to regain our balance and maintain it is within us in the very moment we are experiencing.

It is our divine birthright to live healthy, happy, prosperous lives. This is the balance that you and I are seeking. But we sometimes hinder ourselves by focusing our attention in the wrong direction. Too often we search for the answers to life's riddles in the external world. We are forever looking outside ourselves, seeking approval and striving to impress others. But living to please others is a poor substitute for self-love, for no matter how family and friends may

Everything you require to live in balance is within you at this very moment.

adore us, they can never satisfy our visceral need to love and honor ourselves.

Making our needs our first priority is difficult for all of us, but it is a particular challenge for women. Early on we learn that we are born to serve, that the needs of others supersede our own. We are taught that sacrifice and selflessness are virtues that make us worthy and win us love. But though charity is an expression of divinity, it is a *human* virtue, not the reserve or obligation of women alone. Whether we are female or male, we must not allow the relentless demands of family and work to override our critical need for self-nurturing. When we fail to nurture ourselves, our joy is depleted and our capacity to serve diminished. Giving from an empty vessel causes stress, anger and resentment, seeds that sow disorder and disease. Attempting to meet the demands of the world without first attending to our own needs is an act of self-betrayal that can cause us to lose respect for our value and worth. It is not enough to be kind: We must learn to be kind *and* wise.

Living in balance is vital to our well-being. Without balance, much of the beauty and grandeur of our existence is lost. But a balanced life doesn't just happen. It is a state of grace we create by staying connected with our thoughts and feelings and consciously measuring what we do. Just as feel-

ing fit and flexible demands physical exercise, just as expanding your mind requires intellectual effort, so bringing your life into balance and maintaining your spiritual equilibrium require focused awareness and daily retreat from the stresses of the world.

The wisdom and strength you seek await you in the silence within. Awakening to our deepest desires, to our needs and to our truth requires reflection and inner listening. We must create the space in our lives where our physical self and our spiritual being can meet. The more we nourish our internal world, the more powerful we grow in the external world. Retreating doesn't free us from the concerns of the external world, but it delivers us from the pain of living in it.

Look to the light within you. It's awaiting your attention, longing for your return. You may have lost sight of your inner radiance as you turned to look outside yourself for validation and meaning. You may have forgotten it as you gave authority not to your own inner voice, but to the dictates and opinions of others. Yet no matter how far you wander or how long you stay away, the divine light never flickers or dims. You are host to the eternal flame. It glows in the silence of your being to illumine your life and light your way. The tempests of the world can never eclipse or snuff it out—just as you don't diminish the light of the sun

God never closes one door without opening another.

by pulling down the shades. The radiance within us is always shining, and solitude opens wide the way.

We would probably be more zealous about retreating from the world if it were a complicated task, requiring great effort. But, in fact, the task could not be simpler, because there is nowhere to go, nothing to do. To retreat, you need only *be*. How? By giving yourself to yourself before you give yourself away. It's amazing how a simple fifteen minutes or more of quiet inner listening each day creates such abundant peace and joy. My life works beautifully when I start each day in communion, when I draw a warm bath, lace the water with fragrant oils—frankincense, jasmine, lavender or patchouli—light a single candle and retreat. During this precious time, the tiny bathroom in my small Manhattan apartment becomes a grand and healing space for me.

Choose your place. Any place that's quiet and where you feel completely comfortable—your bed, an easy chair, a mat on the floor—will do. Stretch fully for a few seconds from head to toe before you settle in. Sitting or lying down, close your eyes gently. Allow yourself to breathe slowly, deeply, exhaling longer than you inhale. As you exhale, feel yourself letting go. Consciously relax each part of your body separately, starting with your feet. Tense and tighten them as you inhale. Release and relax them as you exhale. Continue to breathe deeply and fully as you tense and tighten your calves, thighs and buttocks, then your torso, your arms, your shoulders and face. Is there any tightness in the areas where stress normally takes hold—your upper back and shoulders, your neck and jaw? Breathe deeply into each of these areas as you tighten and release those muscles again. Let go completely.

Stay with your breath, breathing slowly, deeply and rhythmically, consciously inhaling joy and peace and exhaling stress and strain. Feel yourself descending deeper and deeper into your breath. You are completely at ease, your body limp and relaxed. Listen to the rhythm of your breath whispering in the stillness. This is the Holy Spirit, the breath of life in you. You are now in touch with your inner light. Feel the love, the peace at the center of your being. Feel its healing light caressing you, filling you, renewing you. Feel its glow enveloping you and radiating from you. This is your own loving-kindness, embracing and restoring you to wholeness.

Now is the time for asking questions of yourself—and for listening for your deepest, most intuitive responses. You need only attune your ear. There is no problem too trivial or concern too great to bring to the spirit within. God resides within you for this very purpose. In this place you can lay your burdens down. So surrender your worries and fears, releasing them into the care of your own inner wisdom.

Give yourself to yourself before you give yourself away.

Continually questioning ourselves is essential to making wise and conscious choices throughout the many stages of our life's journey. We should periodically pause in silence to ask: *What is my purpose here?* We must answer this to stay true to our path. And there are other questions: *Who am I? Do I feel happy, healthy and whole? How can I expand the promise of my life? Have I erected defenses and barriers that are limiting my vision? Am I making choices that encourage my growth? Am I kind to myself? Am I loving to myself? Am I living my truth?* Some of the answers to your questions and challenges will come swiftly; others are revealed over time. But God will never fail to inspire and guide you. Have faith and don't try to hurry spirit. The answers always come at the right time.

When you are ready, open your eyes. Remain still for a moment and experience how at peace you feel. You may feel a smile from your very center. Try to hold on to the tranquil point of light glowing within as you move through the day.

Soon you'll discover the lasting faith and understanding that result from the simple act of listening to yourself in silence each day. It may even seem miraculous. As you honor your need for an intimate relationship with your spirit, you learn to trust in yourself and your inner wholeness. You gain clarity and insight into the people and things that enhance or hamper you. You learn to use your gifts wisely, to set your own standards. You begin to see how life works, how it is always deconstructing and reconstructing itself and always for our higher good.

Transitions in your life become easier now that you are better able to guide them, better able to enjoy the benefits and rewards of change. As you take time to reflect on your life, you see that every challenge along the way offers you another piece of life's puzzle. You recognize that every occurrence in life has its purpose. As you grow in wisdom and faith, you learn to trust life more and discover one of its greatest truths: that God never closes one door without opening another. In the silence, we allow God to lead us to the newly opened doors.

This truth was reinforced for me during a trip I made to Los Angeles. I was there to give a talk about the transformation that is possible when we listen in silence to our spirit. My visit took place just a few months after the devastating earthquake that struck the area in the early morning of January 17, 1994. Just as I was about to leave the ballroom where I'd spoken, a tall, amply endowed woman stepped into my path. I will always remember the joy in her face as she gently clasped my hand.

"Girl, I could have given that same speech you gave tonight," she said, beaming. "I know the great power in the silence." She went on to tell me that she had lost everything

she owned in the earthquake. "Every button, every dish, my house, my car, my job—all gone," she emphasized, "but I'm happy." I was astonished that her spirit was so buoyant despite her loss, and I asked her to tell me about it. She described the chilling experience of being at home alone and jolted awake by the intensity of the earthquake and the violent roar of everything breaking apart around her. In the dark, she had been able to scramble under an archway just as the windows and the ceiling of her home came crashing in. In seconds everything she had worked all her life to acquire was turned into rubble. Much later she would discover a mound of concrete and plaster where her bed had stood.

When the earth finally stopped shuddering, she lay under the archway, amid the debris. She was trapped. And she was terrified that at any moment she could be crushed to death. She lay there crying and calling into the darkness, but no one came. She had always been a high-energy person who orchestrated everything, she told me, and being trapped there for what seemed like hours was pure torture for her. But as she calmed down, she realized she'd better listen for neighbors or rescue workers calling out to her. As she focused her attention on listening, the only sound she heard was the constant rhythm of her breathing in the still, dark morning. Incredibly, she began to relax. The steadiness of her breath became her comfort, her companion, a reminder that she was blessed to be alive. She said that a calm came over her, and for the first time in her life she felt protected and at peace. In the deepest part of her being, she knew she had nothing to fear, for whether or not she was rescued, she had finally found her freedom. In time she heard the sirens and the voices of people calling to her, and as they dug in to reach her, she was able to assure them that, except for a few cuts and bruises, she was just fine.

"Before the quake, I had all the trappings of success," she told me, "but my life was out of balance. I was on a see-saw with too much weight on one side. All the fun had gone out of the ride." But now her priorities had shifted into place, and she was making dramatic changes in her life. "I was unhappy because I was clinging to the things in my life and always wanting more. My home, my job, my clothes, a relationship—I thought they were my security, though they never made me feel secure," she explained. "It took an earthquake and losing everything I owned for me to discover that my security has been with me all along. There is a power within us that we can depend upon no matter what is happening around us. And it is more sure," she laughed, "than the earth beneath our feet." She added thoughtfully, "Now, each day of my life, I take the time to sit in silence and allow God to be God in me."

This woman's story underscores a lesson I hope never

to forget: Listening in the silence each day isn't a luxury, but a necessity. In the stillness of our being there is free-flowing wisdom greater than language can describe. It is a realm of consciousness beyond mind, emotion and personality. In the silence, we are awakened and reattuned to our divinity. When we take quiet time each day, we feel at one with the spirit; if at times we feel the earth shifting beneath us, we know which way to turn. We know to listen in the silence to the sweet small voice that always reminds us: *Be still and know that I am God.*

I Will:
Claiming Your
Power to
Choose

I will are two of the most powerful words we can utter. Words that were in the Beginning. Words through which the Creator created worlds. *I will.* They are both a powerful declaration and a command. They affirm dominion. Take a moment and whisper them to yourself. *I will.* Feel the power. To will is to take the first step. To will is to unleash the divinity within you. Your will is your greatest strength. It is God-power, the power to create that lies within you. Implicit in the words *I will* is the declaration that you have the power to choose. *I will.* An affirmation that you are not inherently weak or inadequate, but inherently strong and complete.

I will has become a powerful mantra for me. *I will.* Words I use to encourage myself to complete difficult tasks and to focus my energy on the many good things I want to bring forth. A conversation I had with my friend Pat Martin one Sunday afternoon reminded me of this powerful creative force within us. It was the day I told Pat that Khephra and I were getting married. It had been nineteen years since my first marriage had ended, and during that time I had done a lot of learning and unlearning, discovering ways to take some of that nurturing support I seemed always to have for others and direct it toward *me.* As I began to take better care of myself, I could see the power I had within me to realize my dreams and goals, and to choose the shape and direction my life would take.

High on my wish list was marriage with a loving partner. I had been down that road once before, and the journey had been a painful one. But this time I knew it would be different. I wasn't looking for deliverance from anything or salvation in anyone. A love relationship was my *choice*, not my need. Pat was so happy for me. *I* was so happy for me. The two of us giggled like girls.

Pat and I have been sisterfriends for decades. We were just eleven and twelve when we met, and through our teens

and into maturity we've been present in each other's lives. Whenever I think about my cherished friendship with Pat, the past is reborn. Through the years we've shared our innermost truths and desires, and Pat was one of the few people who knew how truly important having a special relationship was to me. "You got your wish," Pat exclaimed when I announced my plans to wed. "You've always said you would get married again."

Looking back, I can see that over the nineteen years I had been single, a transformation had taken place in me. As I stopped playing the blame game and started taking responsibility for myself, dealing with myself honestly and compassionately, so many of the blessings I had longed for began to unfold for me. My personal successes encouraged my faith, boosted the expectations I had for myself and increased my enthusiasm for life and its endless possibilities.

As I began trusting and listening to myself more and adopting more life-affirming habits, my career, my income and my happiness increased. As I became more inner-directed, everything got better in my world. I experienced the wonderful feeling of awakening to life's lessons. I could see how embracing these lessons and bringing them forward shapes our future—and I decided that I wanted the divine right man in mine. Being faithful to myself and my desires had fulfilled a lot of dreams and created a lot of sweetness

in my life, and now I wanted the icing on the cake: I wanted someone to share my joy with, to build with, to be with.

The Holy Spirit longs to give us everything that will contribute to our highest good, and I believed I had reached a point where marriage would be good for me. I knew that I would grow in marriage, that it would add another dimension to my life, that the gifts and talents I have to offer would be amplified in a sacred union. I had faith that God would support me in my desire, but I had to do my part. I had to pluck some weeds and clear the ground so that a good relationship could take root and flourish. And so I got busy. I took that desire to the altar within where all the answers lie.

One important insight that became clear to me during my quiet time is that we attract people who reflect where we are in consciousness. That meant I had to love and value myself more and stay true to what is important to me. Spirit also revealed that I had already missed many opportunities for love because they hadn't come in pretty packages. An essential lesson I had to learn is that our gifts are always on the inside and that my focus should be on the heart and the soul of a man and not on how he appears to the world. I also learned that our special angels will not be revealed to us until we have the awareness to recognize them—and the wisdom to treat them with reverence and respect. I had work to

Your greatest hopes and dreams are the blessings that Spirit longs to bestow on you.

do. Rather than trying to find the divine right man, I needed to prepare the way by becoming a divine right person.

When we engage our will and listen inwardly, paying attention to the lessons life offers and committing ourselves to doing the inner work necessary, all the good we desire flows toward us. That is the promise of God within us. The blessings we want don't necessarily come overnight. I had been longing—and preparing myself—for that special relationship for a decade before it happened. But when I was ready, it came, and as with all things, it happened right on time.

If you could realize your most cherished hopes and dreams, what would your choices be? Health and fitness? Financial freedom? A better job? Your own business? A home? A loving partner? A family? All the good things you yearn for are simply God speaking to your heart. Your most imaginative hopes and dreams are the blessings that spirit is longing to unfold through you. Your grandest dreams are all within your reach. If it weren't so, God wouldn't have put the desire so deeply in your soul.

The abundance we want is closer to being realized than most of us might think. All the good that we are seeking is already ours in formless energy. It exists in a state that religious writer Gabriele Wittek calls "prematerial substance," just waiting for us to say yes by doing the work that will bring it into existence. There are no dreams too great to dream, no ambitions or goals too lofty to achieve. We have the inner vision, wisdom and strength to create the life we want, if we will. But most of us unwittingly sell ourselves short by adopting self-limiting behavior that can only produce a limited life.

We are so much more than we seem. We are more than flesh and blood and organs and bones. Each of us is God's living enterprise, a physical expression of the divinity that created us. But our divine potential is meaningless if we are unaware of it. Few of us have an awareness of how precious and powerful we are and of all the blessings life has in store for us. Years ago, before Oprah Winfrey's phenomenal rise, she shared with me that at a point in her life she realized that God wanted more for her than she wanted for herself. "And that made me lift up my faith and my vision," she said. Her understanding of this fundamental truth, along with hard work and attention to detail, opened the way for her talent to soar.

Everything we need to experience a rich and meaningful life is flowing toward us in a full and complete way. So why not do the work to catch it? Why stand under Niagara Falls with only a thimble in your hand?

How do we begin tapping into all this abundance? The place to start is right where you are at this very moment. It's

easy to make excuses for putting off pursuing a richer life: *The kids . . . No time . . . No money . . . I'm too old, too young . . . Maybe next year . . .* But this is the blessed moment. You have everything you need right now to let you take the next step toward realizing your dreams, no matter how small that step may be.

Even the least motivated person possesses the power to choose to live fully and abundantly. We aren't stuck in any relationship, job or living condition that robs us of our joy. It's only the fear that we can't do better that anchors us to a painful place. Fear is our only enemy, our chain to misery and heartache. Fear keeps us focused on what we don't want rather than on what we must do to create peace, abundance and joy. Being fearful is like living in a prison without locks. We can open the gates and step into the light any time we choose. We must have the will and the courage to guard against negative thinking and to make room for positive, life-supporting thoughts.

I will! Proclaim it to yourself and mean it. *I will aim arrows of achievement at my fears. I will broaden my perspective. I will add depth and meaning to my life.* Look beyond your city and beyond this country. We are citizens of the world. Deny any limiting beliefs you hold and start planning for what you wish for and deserve. Such is God's great love for us that at each and every moment we can exercise our power to choose.

For years I delayed enrolling in college because other people insisted I didn't need a degree. Even close friends who I know love me and have my best interests at heart discouraged me from going back to school. I was already at the top of my career, they said. I was making more money than many people with advanced degrees. "Don't let insecurity make you feel you need a degree," they would offer. "You're doing just fine. Read books. Everything you need to know is in the library." Good advice, but these suggestions weren't truths for me. I need structure and deadlines, or I never get the job done. Furthermore, I felt like a fraud: I knew that I needed more education and information so that I could be more proficient in the job I already had.

Even the wonderful man who was in my life at that time—he had a law degree and an M.B.A., and his intellect was a major influence in my decision to go to college—reminded me that I was already too busy with the magazine and my daughter: School, he said, would only take more time from our relationship. But I wanted to prepare myself to do great things in the future, to be a help, not a burden, to the community—I didn't want to spend my elder years as a poor Black woman, the most vulnerable among our elderly. So I enrolled in school and took classes during the day, evening, weekends and summers, and I hung in there until I graduated. I'll be forever grateful that I listened to my

own heart and not to anyone else's advice. No one knows better what's best for us than we do. No one cares about our well-being more than we do. And that's the way it should be.

We are creative beings, and God is always offering us creative ideas that we can act upon to liberate and fulfill ourselves. We all procrastinate to some degree. But as in any other area of our lives, we can choose to change this behavior the moment we decide it is a form of self-sabotage in which we will no longer indulge.

Take notes on your visions and dreams—it's one of the ways you lock them in. Sometimes we don't act on our most valuable ideas simply because we've forgotten them! I make it a rule never to go anywhere, not to dinner or to a concert or a picnic, without a pen and paper tucked away. Creativity is always streaming forth, and I want to be there to catch it. I learned this lesson the hard way: If I don't write it down, it's as good as gone.

Keep a special notebook that can serve as your life's agenda, and refer to it every day. Keep it simple: Divide it into two sections, one for daily tasks, the other for long-range plans. Use a daily planner or a plain spiral pad. A book of any size with bound pages will do. On the daily to-do side, keep a running list of the little things you must do to manage your life. Prioritize the tasks and eliminate the

things that are time wasters or unimportant. Whatever doesn't get done today is placed on tomorrow's list.

A major section of your personal agenda should be devoted to your life list. This is where you note, in order of priority, your most cherished desires and goals. Your life list is more than words on paper. It is a compass, a road map you must read and reread frequently—adjusting, correcting, refining and refocusing as you gain clarity. This is a blueprint of your life's major themes. Starting with your top priority, break your goal down into the smallest component parts and begin to add one or two of those tasks to your daily agenda. My old buddy Reverend Ike would preach this in his motivational sermons all the time: "Inch by inch, anything is a cinch!" I thought it silly then; now I know that it's true.

If feeling healthy and strong is a major goal, you might move to your daily to-do sheet some of the small, simple measures you must commit yourself to in order to be fit. Your notes to yourself might include a reminder to schedule your important medical exams, to set aside time for exercise, to take your vitamins and have a fruit or vegetable plate for lunch. I must always remind myself to do my breast self-examination each month, to drink lots of water and to walk for forty-five minutes each day. If having your own business is one of your greatest dreams, you help bring it to fruition

by making notes to schedule meetings with people in your industry of choice and by signing up for a course on start-up ventures. No company operates efficiently without a business plan. No person operates effectively without a life plan.

Envisioning, planning and list making, however, are only part of the process. The reality is that we will get out of life only what we work to achieve. You may have a burning desire to become a writer, a performer, a doctor or an entrepreneur, but there is nothing that God can do to help you without *your* help. *You* must choose to take action. *You* must choose to discipline yourself, to stretch yourself and launch your dream. Don't look for miracles to change bad habits: There is no miracle that will change us. God doesn't do the work for us, but through us. We must choose to change, to act in our own behalf.

Everyone yearns for a better life. Yet few people take even the smallest steps in that direction. We can easily keep treading down that same old beaten path that leads only to a place we neither want nor need to be in. My wise teacher Eric Butterworth says that the *desire* to do is proof positive of the *potential* to do. We must make the commitment to take the steps to break out of our inertia. All that's needed, Eric says, is the conscious application of mental effort to redirect our course. A right-thinking mind can actually propel us in

the direction we need to go. But the impetus to change direction, to adopt a more life-affirming course, must come first and must originate within ourselves. We have the power to reverse our mental gears and live abundantly. But first we must choose to act.

We bring about positive change by actively cultivating a positive attitude that shapes our thoughts, words and deeds. Like Oprah, we must choose to lift our faith and our vision. It's easy to feel motivated when we're listening to an inspiring sermon, or the choir is praising God in song, but the real work begins when the temple doors close behind you. You must become the guardian of your thoughts and actions. It's imperative that you surround yourself with positive people—those who affirm you and show by their words and deeds that they like you and believe in your dreams. Don't even allow yourself to utter the words *I can't*. Delete them from your vocabulary. And every time a negative thought comes into your mind, pluck it out, toss it away and replace it with a positive idea. This is not easy, but it's doable and necessary if we are to move ourselves and our communities forward. Our parents and grands brought us this far by believing that they could and by holding fast to their dreams. Moment to moment you must practice staying on the good foot, and in time your positive thinking and optimism will become as natural to you as breathing.

Your mind is a prolific author; what you believe composes your life.

When I was making space in my life for my divine right man, I turned my back on the parade of women who make a habit of putting Black men down. I love my brothers, always have. I see good men wherever I am because that is the feeling I hold in my heart. Faith has tremendous power, and it works either way: Our negative or positive faith helps shape our future. The vision you keep, the words you speak pave the way for your experiences. The mind is a prolific author. What you believe—along with the action you take—composes your life. At this moment our lives reflect where we have been in consciousness and what we have done with our time.

The creative process is always at work in you, giving you whatever you expect and work passionately toward. When you believe in something, you create a pathway for receiving it. If you believe life is great, you see great possibilities, you plan for them and, through your actions, you produce them. If you are doubtful and fearful, you shun opportunities, you limp through life, and everything you touch turns to dust.

The divine intelligence that supports all creation is fixed and unchanging. A spark of that infinite wisdom resides within you, at the center of your being, waiting to do your bidding. Even if you feel you have messed up your life, no matter how off course you may be, at any time you

choose, you can get back on your path again. We all have regrets; I know I have mine. But the past is gone, the future is unformed, and how we choose to use this day will determine what our future will be.

The path to realizing our dreams is never smooth. Invariably we encounter bends, turns, detours and roadblocks. Sometimes our frustrations make us want to give up the journey, but frustrations signal the need to pause for introspection and redirection. Frustrations are promptings from God to search our souls even more deeply to find our power and purpose, and to live it. Frustrations tell us that our thoughts and actions are not yet in harmony with our desires. We will always feel unfulfilled, fragmented and frustrated unless we commit ourselves to continuous growth and change.

That is part of the divine plan. Until we bring into balance our activities and our capabilities, we will feel the frustration of working against life. Thank God! The frustration we feel from not realizing our potential isn't a punishment but a blessing, a self-correcting mechanism. If I could feel fit, focused and happy overeating and sitting in front of the TV, I'd never move a muscle. But when I stuff my face and give up my fitness regimen, my belly grows bigger than my butt and my thoughts get muddled. I know that I will alle-

viate my frustration by getting back on track and choosing what's best for me again.

There simply are no valid excuses for giving up and not going the distance in our lives. Julyette Matthews Marshall, who today lives in Houston, is a powerful reminder that no matter how frustrated we may feel or how monumental our challenges may be, we have the power to keep moving forward. Julyette was born in the little oil-refinery town of Port Arthur, Texas, about ninety miles southeast of Houston. When she was five days old, a physician, the man she believes was her biological father, and his wife, the local grammar-school principal, adopted her. "It was never a secret that my birth mother was a young woman in our town," she recalls. "For a while, she would visit me on Sundays, but she moved away when I was around six." Julyette's father, who was fifty when she was born, adored his little girl. "He would tell me often that I was chosen," she remembers. But there was always tension between her and her adoptive mother. "The circumstances of my birth put a tremendous strain on the marriage," she explains.

But despite the circumstances of her birth, Julyette, the couple's only child, remembers having a charmed life. She was popular and a natural athlete. She became a lifeguard, a majorette, part of the drill team and the youngest girl to

65

play varsity basketball. After high school, she attended Fisk University in Nashville and then accepted a teaching position at Southern University in Baton Rouge, where she met her husband. They had a daughter, Nikki, but after two years the marriage ended, and Julyette moved back to Texas with the baby. She was doing fine, working for the U.S. Department of Labor and taking care of her little girl, when she was hit with an emotional doubleheader.

In 1977, Julyette broke up with a man she had intended to marry when she discovered he had battered his former wife. That same year, her beloved father passed away. "Daddy was the first person close to me to die," Julyette says. "He was my heart. Losing him and my relationship at the same time was devastating. I needed a change, so when a friend suggested I try California, I packed up my belongings, and Nikki and I moved there." She enrolled her daughter in school, found an apartment and a job, and was beginning to settle in when her life was turned upside down yet again.

One night Julyette was awakened by a severe backache. "It felt like a horse had kicked me in the middle of my back," she remembers. "I took lots of aspirin, but I couldn't lie still. I paced the floor all night." Nikki was excited about going on a weeklong class trip to the mountains, and Julyette was determined to get her daughter to the bus station

in the morning. The back pain had subsided, but Julyette felt so weak after dropping Nikki off that she decided to stay home from work that day to rest. "Within a couple of hours I couldn't bend my legs," she remembers. "I pulled myself together and went to a chiropractor, who thought I might have a pinched nerve." But after several days, when things hadn't settled down, a friend took Julyette to the hospital at the University of California in Los Angeles. "When I walked in, nothing was hurting," she recalls. "But my legs were just so stiff."

Doctors probed and tested her for hours, from four o'clock that afternoon until three the following morning. Julyette says prayer got her through that night. The next morning the nurses and doctors gathered around her, but when they asked Julyette to sit up, she couldn't. The medical team was not surprised that paralysis had set in: "They told me that I would be completely paralyzed for the rest of my life," she remembers.

Julyette was thirty-five years old. She was a woman on the move. She drove a blue sports car, played tennis, rollerskated, swam. "I was good at everything physical," she says. The doctor's diagnosis, transverse myelitis, a sudden inflammation of the spinal cord that is sometimes a precursor to multiple sclerosis, didn't even begin to sink in. She asked the nurse to just give her a pill and let her go home. Nikki

would be returning from her camping trip, and Julyette had to be at the bus station to pick her up. "They thought I'd had a nervous breakdown," Julyette says. "A psychiatrist came in and asked if I wanted to commit suicide. I said, 'How could I? Someone would have to roll me over to the window and push me out.' They couldn't comprehend why I wasn't devastated." She was still focused on getting home and preparing for Nikki, even though she was completely paralyzed from the neck down.

For the next eight months, "home" for Julyette Marshall was the Daniel Freeman Rehabilitation Center in Los Angeles. "I was helpless," she says. "I couldn't even swat a fly. I remember one day, at a time when I couldn't even move my head, a fly was on my face and I started to cry, hoping my tears would move it." But Julyette has a will of iron. She refused to accept the doctors' prognosis. "I was determined to walk again. My mind was trained on going home to Nikki, who was ten years old and staying with friends. I needed to be at home with her," she recalls.

The doctor in charge would dismiss her constant requests to go home by telling her he would sign her out if she could walk. That was all Julyette needed to hear. *God, you said, "Ask and you shall receive,"* she remembers saying to herself one day before asking the nurse in the physical-therapy room to push her wheelchair over to the stairs. "It took me

three hours, but with the sweat rolling off my body, I made it up those three little steps," Julyette says. "The doctor didn't believe me, but when the nurse confirmed it, he said, 'This may cost me my license, but I'll sign you out.' The three of us were in tears."

It was her faith in the divine life force working on her side that helped her up those stairs, Julyette states emphatically. "God said, 'Trust Me, and I'll make it possible.' And I believed." Within six months her toes began to move involuntarily. "Then it felt as if my arms were thawing out," she says. "When you're paralyzed you don't have a menstrual cycle, and one day I felt dampness in the bed. By that time Nikki and I were back in Texas, and the doctor who was working with me said it was a great sign. Little by little this thawing-out process continued, and the paralysis eventually disappeared."

Today Julyette uses a wheelchair, but the paralysis is completely gone. "I only have lower-body weakness; my legs are heavy all the time. But I can cross my legs and wiggle my toes, and when I have the money for intensive therapy I know I will walk again," she declares, adding reflectively, "Paralysis is a time when you are truly by yourself. But it was a special time. I realized that God is everything. It was just the two of us."

The night I met Julyette, she had come alone to a re-

ception at Houston's Nia Gallery because a friend she expected to bring her didn't show up. She wanted to talk to me about promoting her Afrocentric accessories and imported African crafts. Through her small company, Zamaani, Julyette has formed a business relationship with a team of physically challenged elders and children who live in a village in Kenya and supply her with crafts they make. The gift shop at The African American Museum in Dallas sells some of her imports. "They don't even know who I am," Julyette chuckles. "I send them a box of crafts, and they send me a check. I'm the CEO, the PR person, the salesperson and the secretary. I'm aggressive because I have to be. But I don't want to get on people's nerves in my effort to promote my business, so I have a couple of voices I use over the phone. No one is coming to my door, so I do what I must to be heard." When I marvel at her strength, courage and tenacity, she brushes off my admiration and laughs, "I'm amazed myself at what I can do from the center of my bed."

Julyette Matthews Marshall is a powerful reminder of how far we can go when we lift our vision and our faith. The vision we hold of ourselves and of what we can achieve is everything. How we see ourselves and our world determines our identity, our behavior and the choices we make each day. We must refuse to see ourselves as victims, no matter what challenges we face. We are not limited by racism, sex-

ism, ageism or any abuse that may have occurred in our lives. Julyette's life is proof that no challenge can diminish our spirit, that nothing is more powerful than a mind made up. The simple declaration *I will* is the beginning of all our triumphs.

Remember, life is for living and learning. So listen to your life and the lessons it offers. What choices must you make this day to help you move forward? Make your list of the things you can do right now to create what you want and begin to do the work. You *can* say yes to happiness, wholeness and prosperity. You *can* live fully and creatively. You *can* claim your power to choose. Why not claim it now?

Living in the
Moment

It seems not long ago that I was in my twenties. Now, amazingly, my daughter is. How quickly the days of our lives seem to pass. The seasons and the years appear to hurry by, but in fact it is we who create a past and a future, because only we measure time. We often say time flies, when it is we who are flying forward, our bodies in one place but our minds far down the road.

Time is the eternal now, but *our* world is one of ceaseless activity. We are always on the move. Often we live in

fast-forward mode, racing against the clock. Sometimes we find ourselves rushing through our days—eating fast, speaking fast, walking at breakneck speed. At times I rush about with such intensity it must look to others as if someone is chasing me. And before long I find myself battling another case of the crazies: first the little twitch in the outer corner of my left eye, then the days when I find myself snapping at folks, and the nights when sleep won't come. Every emotion and mental attitude we are host to creates after its kind. So when we forget to stay centered, our bodies begin to weaken, our thoughts become confused, our words are less careful, our decisions less sure. We become magnets for the very physical and emotional ailments we most want to avoid—and all because we are letting the world sweep us along on its rushing tide, rather than experiencing and enjoying the moments of our lives.

Each moment is magical, precious and complete and will never exist again. We forget that *now* is the moment we are in, that the next one isn't guaranteed. And if we are blessed with another moment, any joy, creativity or wisdom it brings will ensue from the way we live the present one.

Like all of life's lessons, this one is sublime in its simplicity, yet sometimes so difficult to put into practice—particularly during times when we are under stress. For most of us, the year-end holiday season is a pressured time. No mat-

ter how often we promise ourselves that we're not going to rush or push ourselves to the point of exhaustion, it rarely works out that way.

Last Thanksgiving weekend I got caught up in the frenzy once again. Simply put, I had too much on my plate. There was writing to do, manuscripts to review, a book tour to begin and the editorial budget and year-end reports due at work. My husband, Khephra, and I had decided to go upstate to the country for a working holiday. My daughter would spend the weekend with her father, my sister, Lillian, with her honey's family. Any guilt I felt at not being, for the first time, with the family on Thanksgiving was offset by my relief at not having to do supermarket or kitchen duty. But I still had so much to do before Khephra and I could get away. Lillian wanted us to visit our mother's grave to clean it and place fresh flowers there. I also had to buy food to take upstate, and make sure that my elderly Uncle Arnold would have an enjoyable Thanksgiving meal.

I had planned to leave the office at one-thirty, go home to get the car, shop for food, buy flowers, then stop by Sylvia's restaurant in Harlem for a down-home meal I knew Uncle Arnold would love. Then I would pick up Lil and get to the cemetery before closing time at four. But none of these things worked out as planned.

I was delayed at the office and wasn't able to leave un-

til two-forty-five. *Not to worry,* I thought. *I'll just pick up the car, get Lil and the flowers and take care of everything else after visiting Mommy's grave.* But I dashed home to find that the car wasn't there. The garage attendant said that Khephra had taken the car about an hour earlier. I was fuming. After all, I had told Khephra of my plans. But where there's a will, there's a way, right? So I hopped in a taxi and was pulling out of my building's driveway when Khephra came cruising in. Suffice it to say I could have handled my sweetie's forgetfulness with a lot more kindness and grace. I jumped out of the cab, grabbed the car from Khephra and was headed on my way. I could still get to the cemetery if I hurried. It was about three-fifteen when I turned out of my street onto Central Park West—and into a sea of traffic.

I had forgotten the nightmare that Manhattan traffic is before any holiday weekend, when offices close early and folks are scurrying to make their exodus from the city. Half an hour later, at three-forty-five, I was still sitting in traffic about six blocks from my home with my teeth clenched, my head pounding and tears rolling down my cheeks.

I was exhausted. Tired of being on call everywhere. It seemed every moment of my life was scheduled. Overscheduled. It was all too much for me. That Wednesday afternoon, stuck in holiday traffic, I cried to myself: *Why do I have so many responsibilities?* And from within me came the re-

Each moment is magical, precious and complete and will never exist again.

sponse: *You have so many responsibilities because you are responsible. And your health and sanity depend on your handling your responsibilities and not allowing them to handle you.*

I am continually amazed by the power of God in us. The wisdom of the spirit is always so near. At that moment, God's temple was stuck in traffic, but the spirit dwells even there. In the instant that I recognized that truth, I felt myself renewed. My tension and tears gave way to peace and joy. I even laughed from a grateful heart. All at once I saw my responsibilities as what they are—my life's many blessings. I felt thankful to be needed instead of needy. And I realized that I could put myself in charge of my life and not become overwhelmed.

I saw that even if I had left the office on time, there was no way I could have completed all the chores I had committed myself to in the amount of time I had allotted. Once again I had assigned tasks to myself that didn't have to be mine and that I certainly didn't have to attend to all in one day. I saw that at any time I choose, I can take things off my agenda, reprioritize and change my schedule around. The trip to the cemetery was my sister's pilgrimage, not mine. For me, Mommy is not in the cemetery. She lives in my heart. And Sylvia's restaurant doesn't close till ten-thirty at night—I still had more than six hours to pick up Uncle Arnold's Thanksgiving dinner. And the supermarket stays

open twenty-four hours. I had let my mind run in every direction, fretting and fussing, trying to orchestrate an afternoon that was obviously not meant to be. Rather than feeling angry and overwhelmed because events weren't working out the way I had planned, I realized that I could actually sit amid honking horns and impatient drivers and experience the serenity in each holy moment. I saw that I was frustrating myself needlessly—saw how, with a simple change of attitude, a perfect peace could be mine.

I calmly picked up the car phone, called my sister and let her know that we weren't going to make it to the cemetery that day, but that I would still come by. Only now I was taking my time. Then I called Khephra to apologize for the angry way I had seized the car. And as it turned out, Lillian, my little niece Sahara and I had a perfectly wondrous evening, flowing in slow motion with the holiday traffic, attending to our errands, listening to music and remembering Mommy. That evening I reaped the rewards of choosing to live in each moment and stay centered in my life.

Life is for living, not for rushing through. We are meant to experience each moment fully, to savor each second, for that is where our peace and power lie. Haste, tension and frustration are habits that rob us of our joy.

At any moment something is going on that can make us feel pressured and tense. People push past us while we're

waiting in line. Troublesome coworkers cause us grief. The plane, the train, the bus are late or canceled. Anything can happen—but we must forever guard against letting it happen *in us*. We can't control what happens out there in the world, but we can put ourselves in charge of our inner world. There will never be a time when we can't find something to worry about—but there will also never be a time when we can't choose to stop worrying.

We learn to accept tension, thinking it's a natural part of our lives. We learn to rush, fuss and fear and can easily find ourselves storming through each day. And if we don't take care, huffing and puffing and screaming and shouting can easily become a part of our identity—the usual way we respond to the day's challenges.

Panic in the face of adversity is a learned response. Here's how to unlearn it: Surrender to your breath. Surrendering to your breath is surrendering to God. Try it wherever you are right now. Do nothing but breathe deeply for just a minute. Isn't it amazing how much calmer you immediately feel? The little stingy breaths we live on each day sap our energy and exacerbate stress and strain. Instead, relax and inhale deeply. Now give it back. Do it again and again. This is how God intended you to breathe each breath, inhaling and exhaling fully within each moment, not just when you retreat from the world for quiet time, prayer

or meditation. Breathing deeply helps make each moment of your life a prayer. As we experience each inhalation and exhalation fully, we put ourselves in touch with divine order, with the rhythm of life. So keep the deep breathing going. Feel the peace. Come back to it each time you feel yourself stray. Always remember that the source of your tranquillity is within you, at the very center of your being, the place of oneness.

If we would train ourselves to surrender to each breath, we would never feel frantic or fearful. It may sound too simple to be true, but life *is* simple, living each breath is simple—though not easy. We have to practice staying centered from moment to moment.

Deep rhythmic breathing connects you to the life force of the universe. It stakes your claim, your divine right, to be here. With each conscious deep breath, you'll experience the perfect peace and poise at your center, where God dwells, connecting you to the serenity and wisdom within you, and to the peace and power in every moment.

Living fully in the present moment is the key to self-mastery. Breathing deeply helps to center us in the moment by clearing the mind of distractions. But we can also minimize the distractions by simplifying our world. Dispense with clutter in every area of your life. Clean out your drawers and closets, your kitchen cabinets. Look around your

Any joy, creativity or wisdom our next moment brings will ensue from the way we live our present one.

$\mathcal{L}\,i\,v\,i\,n\,g$
$i\,n\quad t\,h\,e$
$\mathcal{M}\,o\,m\,e\,n\,t$

home and give away the things you don't use. Organize your work area. Our happiness isn't bolstered by the things we collect, but by our level of inner peace. Material things come and go; we can live quite comfortably with those things that truly serve a purpose or bring us joy.

Don't permit hordes of people and projects to drain your energy and time. I'm always amazed when folks speak about their ten best friends. Each friendship requires time, energy and commitment. It means being there for another person, consistently offering comfort and care. Do any of us have enough energy or time to take care of ourselves and ten other adults? I know it's not possible for me to have deep and meaningful relationships with that many people at once. It serves your life better if you begin to think of your-self as having ever-widening circles of friends and acquain-tances. Remember, not everyone is healthy enough to have a front-row seat in your life.

Nourish yourself. Make every effort to simplify your diet and not crowd your plate with food. When you com-fort yourself all day by staying calm and centered, you don't rush home feeling frustrated and overwrought and head to the refrigerator for comfort. When you're living harmo-niously, you don't need to count calories: You simply eat when you're hungry. You desire what's good for you, and you have the presence of mind to push yourself away from

the table before you're stuffed. Exercising isn't a chore when you're living in the moment. When you're centered, you're more willing to take the time to discover the exercises you enjoy. And the time you spend strengthening and stretching your body becomes a special time you spend with yourself, a time you begin to look forward to.

Take time for renewal. Even in the small one-bedroom apartment where I raised my daughter, I learned how important it was to take a moment's respite. But I wasn't always so wise. When Nequai was a youngster, most days I'd come racing home from the office completely stressed out. I'd hit the door, step out of my heels and head straight to the kitchen to start dinner, fussing all the while: "Turn off that television! Where is your homework? Did you clean up your room?"

One evening a friend from out of town came home with me after work. After witnessing my madness, he asked if that was how I came home to Nequai every day. Well, I gave that brother fever. I told him I was raising my daughter the way my parents had raised me, and I'd turned out just fine, thank you. I went on and on. But I heard him. And over time, I started coming home from work differently. After hugging and kissing my Pumpkin, I'd ask her to excuse me while I took a few minutes to restore myself. I'd retreat to the quiet of the bathroom and just sit still for a moment.

There I would remind myself to leave the pressures of work at work and to come back to my center. I'd remind myself not to scream and holler, but to be gentle and loving. Before cooking and correcting, I learned to just sit with Nequai for a few minutes and ask her about her day. At first she found it strange that I was even interested. But soon she began to trust my new behavior, and positive changes began to occur in our household. Perhaps for the first time, I felt happy and calm in the evening. I began to look forward to the time for nurturing and rekindling the love within our home. And Nequai grew calmer and happier, too. In time she went from being a failing student to becoming an honor student and eventually the valedictorian of her high-school class.

Feeling connected to the natural world connects us to the rhythms of life. Get away! Any way you can. Walk, drive, take a train or hop on a bus to a peaceful place where you can enjoy the beauty of nature. In the winter, I go skiing with my husband, and while I'm not that anxious to navigate my way down some steep and winding slopes, I love taking the ski lift up to the majestic mountaintop. I am awed when I behold the magnificence that God has created all around us. God's glory is everywhere: in a field of weeds and wildflowers; in the stillness of the woods with the trees arching over us; in a crystal lake lapping softly at the shore; in the rustling of leaves, the scamper of little animals.

If you can't escape to the country, you can still sit at your window and watch the sky. You can watch the rain and the snow. You can visit a nearby park and watch the foliage change with each season. You can turn your face toward the warmth of the sun or feel a gentle breeze whisper against your skin. You can wonder at the changing patterns of light in a summer sky, and feel the brisk tingle of snowflakes in a winter storm. Revel in the knowledge that your senses are finely attuned to these sensations of the natural world. By staying in tune with nature, you nourish the eternal spirit within, you come back to the center of life and to the awareness that God is everywhere present at each moment in time.

Our beloved poet and sage Maya Angelou believes that every few weeks we should take a day off to do absolutely nothing. "What we really have to do is take a day and sit down and think," she shared in a recent interview. "The world is not going to end or fall apart. Jobs won't be lost. Kids will not run crazy in one day. Lovers won't stop speaking to you. Husbands and wives are not just going to disappear. Just take that one day and think. Don't read. Don't write. No television, no radio, no distractions. Sit down and think. . . . Go sit in a church, or in the park, or take a long walk and think. Call it a healing day."

How wise Maya Angelou is. A healing day, a day just

Staying centered in each moment puts you in charge of your life.

to sit and think, a day in which you become still and experience each precious moment of time. By learning to stay centered in the moment, we put ourselves in charge. We experience the joy of living, the wonder in each breath. If we take control of the world within ourselves, no circumstance outside us will have its way with us. When we live moment to moment, we place ourselves at the center of life, where infinite wisdom abides, rather than on the periphery, where things are forever changing and we are susceptible to the vagaries of the world. It is in our awareness each moment of our oneness with God that our inner peace and greatest strength lie.

Just a few weeks after my Thanksgiving Eve experience, when I reconnected with the need to live at the very center of each moment, I faced a challenge that put my spiritual resolution to the test. I was on a cross-country promotional tour for the paperback publication of my first book, *In the Spirit*. My escort, Camilla, had picked me up from my Los Angeles hotel early that morning. I was a guest on several drive-time radio shows, then headed to my hotel for a phone and two print interviews. Three book signings had been scheduled for later in the day.

After the phone and print interviews, I checked out of the hotel because there would be no time to return later to collect my luggage. Against my better judgment, I left all

my belongings in my escort's car during the second book signing. I'll never forget stepping out of the bookstore into the bright California sunshine after the event and discovering the empty space where Camilla's car had been. We looked blankly at each other, incredulous. Camilla had lost her car in a city where, if you mean to do business, a car is a necessity. And I'd lost my jewelry, my winter coat and all the clothes I would need for the three cities I would visit later that week. My laptop computer, disks, the introduction to this book, the package of manuscripts I was to send overnight to the magazine—they were all gone. I stood there in the parking lot with only the clothes I was wearing. At that moment I realized I had a choice. I could either rant and rave, or I could acknowledge a deeper truth, that I had everything I needed within me to keep on stepping. As I stood still, centered in the divinity within, and simply whispered to myself, *Everything is in divine order*, I was amazed at how peaceful, calm and protected I felt. I was able to put my arm around Camilla and reflect on how blessed we were that we hadn't been in the car when it was taken, that we still had ourselves. Looking back, I know that if that loss had occurred on a day when I felt rushed and anxious, my reaction would have been totally different. But all that day, during the many interviews and at the book signings, I had

L i v i n g
i n   t h e
M o m e n t

been talking about the power of the divine within us. I was conscious of living in the spirit, and the spirit carried me through.

Instead of giving my power to panic, I trusted the spirit to provide for me. With a clear mind I was able to take care of business. I made all the necessary calls to report the losses and to let folks know what I needed. Later that evening, when I walked into the Los Angeles airport with nothing in my possession but the clothes on my back, I experienced a curious exhilaration. I felt light and unburdened and centered in the truth that my security is within, that there is no separation between me and God.

The next day I was speaking with Tom Burrell, the Chicago-based advertising wizard who is the founder and CEO of the Burrell Communications Group. Tom has a challenging vision problem: He has very little frontal vision and sees mostly peripherally. As we talked about what had happened to me in Los Angeles, he shared a lesson he had learned long ago that he said has served him well: "I never focus on what I have lost, but on what I have left." Thank you, Tom.

So often we miss the splendor of each moment because we are focused on what we feel we've lost—good health, a relationship, a job, a cherished family member or friend. To

live in the moment, we need to affirm what we have—that we are one with life, one with God. We must trust enough to let go of the past and not worry about what's to come. No matter what is happening in your life, you are in the divine right place and a part of the universal flow. Remember, God is wherever you are; the divine right experiences will unfold, and you will be there to live each moment as it happens.

What are our lives if not the sum of our moments here? We should live each moment with peace and joy. We know this in theory. Now we must make it part of our lives.

Serenity is a gift you receive the instant you begin to dispense with life's clutter and enter fully into each moment, each breath. Practice living in the moment. Make a prayerful sound: *Ashé*. Whisper it to yourself: *Ashé*. This is the ancient Yoruba invocation that asserts our belief in life and in ourselves. It affirms our trust in our inner power and our willingness to surrender our lives to God. *Ashé*. Amen. So be it. The power and the magic within each moment are yours.

Living Love

 L ife is a journey back to God, and our relationships are the road we travel. They are our call to love, our call to discover the Love that is God. They are the path along which we learn to apply the spiritual lessons that are so easy to articulate but so difficult to live.

Our relationships test us. They may cause great upheaval in our lives and shake us to the core. They may lead us to question even our firmest beliefs. At times we will suffer greatly because of them. And when we do, we inevitably

seek someone or something to blame: a world gone mad, others' insensitivity and lack of caring, our own wrong choices. But all upheavals have their purpose: They usher in new beginnings. They rouse us to examine ourselves and our behavior, and prompt us to develop faith and courage, which, without the ravaging effects of hurt and pain, we would never seek. The continuous challenges in our relationships serve to remind us of our purpose in life, which is to grow in love, wisdom and kindness. If we are attentive to the lessons of our relationships, we discover that we, and no one else, are responsible for our happiness and joy.

Spiritual ideas and concepts alone won't bring about change and create the happiness and joy we long for. Only staying aware of and practicing them will. Our relationships give us opportunities to explore the breadth of our own unique being and to become accepting of ourselves, which is the starting place for acceptance of others. Too often in our relationships, we focus on the disruptive behavior of others rather than on our own. But life is biased toward growth, and it invariably draws us to the people and circumstances we need for our highest development. Our most difficult relationships offer us the greatest opportunity for growth and change. Understanding that these challenges are for our spiritual awakening should inspire us to examine vigilantly our own behavior, to explore our own feelings and

Your most difficult relationships offer you the greatest opportunity for growth and change.

responses with compassion and love. By dedicating our-selves to this process of self-discovery, we open the way for a deeply intimate relationship with ourselves. This primary relationship is fundamental to our sense of self-worth and self-acceptance and is the basis for creating loving relation-ships with others.

Our relationships are our sacred responsibilities, for they are the framework within which life is lived. They show us where we have more learning and loving to do. Our interactions with others call up the disabling beliefs and negative patterns of behavior we need to release—the cyn-icism, anger, resentment and jealousy that block love's flow. Our relationships are our mirrors; they reflect where we are in consciousness. And if we are willing to face the truth about ourselves, our relationships offer the lessons that lead to our greatest transformation.

A situation arose with my daughter some time ago that presented me with a deeper understanding of myself. Nequai hadn't honored a family commitment, and I was fu-rious with her. Everything I know about being loving and forgiving was forgotten that day. Khephra and I were up-state at our peaceful mountainside retreat, but there was no sense of peace in me. I was angry, anxiously awaiting Nequai's call. I'd already chosen the words I'd use to shake her, to shame her and blame her for disappointing the fam-

ily. I'd gone over it at least a thousand times in my head. My anger only grew as the hours passed and still I didn't hear from her.

When I couldn't stand the pain of thinking about it any longer, I decided to go for a walk. I stepped out into the crisp fall air sweeping across the Shawangunk Mountains and was abruptly distracted from my fury by the wonder and perfection that surrounded me. The lofty, cotton-white clouds floating majestically above the Hudson Valley and the riot of fall colors covering the land collided with my overcast and stormy disposition. For a moment I completely forgot myself. Revelation, like lightning, strikes when you least expect it. How could I feel so miserable in the midst of such splendor? The question flashed through me all at once, not waiting for words to express it. The answer came more slowly: *No one makes you angry. Anger, like love, is something you choose.* Stunned, I sat down in the middle of the field I'd been walking through. I knew I needed to look within myself, let go of my anger and have a quiet talk with God. When we are hurting deeply, there is always a life lesson we can draw from the experience. I asked the spirit within what I was to learn from this distressing situation, and in the hour or so that I sat quietly listening, I began to see that I was viewing it all wrong.

We are here to love, not to judge. I'd been blaming and

Relationships act as mirrors, reflecting our level of consciousness.

ranting and raging. I certainly wasn't loving Nequai that afternoon as I know God loves me. God's love doesn't insist on perfection or even good common sense. Why then should *I* demand more of those I love? With this tiny change in perspective I began to see that the need for correction wasn't in my daughter, but in me. Nequai is a woman, no longer my little girl; I needed to stop demanding that she live according to my values, to how I wish her to be. To love a person is to support that person in discovering his or her own identity. It's easy for parents to slip into the trap of looking for our wholeness in our children as a substitute for discovering it within ourselves. My expectation that Nequai would conform to my image of perfection—an ideal *I* could never achieve—was born of my own insecurity and self-punishing ego.

I couldn't get home fast enough. I so wanted to share the revelation with Khephra and to reach out to Nequai in this new frame of mind. Charged with energy and unburdened by the anger that had been weighing so heavily on my heart, I twirled and waved my arms in the air, smiling and rejoicing, *Thank you, Lord,* all the way home. I felt that I had taken a giant step forward in my spiritual development.

I hadn't been home fifteen minutes when the telephone rang. Even before I answered, I knew it was Nequai on the line. She told me she'd wanted to speak with me all

day, but had just mustered the courage to call and apologize. I let her know that her instincts were right—that my heart had been closed, but that now it was open.

Love isn't something we give when a person does what we want them to do and withdraw when they don't. Love is a belief system we adopt and strive to live each moment. Nequai and I often remind each other of a lesson Maya Angelou taught us during our stay with her in Winston-Salem. "Even if a person slams the door in your face, you should open it for them," Maya said. We were incredulous and wanted to know why. Maya stated simply, "Because it's never about the other person or their brutish behavior, it's always about *your* spirit and *you* being right with God." Without denying our emotions, we must decide not to let them rule us. Instead of responding emotionally to the differences that create tension in our relationships, we must practice pausing and turning to the wisdom within for understanding and guidance so that we choose to make a loving response. I've found that we greatly reduce the level of frustration and unhappiness we experience in our most intimate relationships if we reduce our many demands to preferences and come to these unions expecting nothing but respect.

The mother-daughter dyad is perhaps the most emotionally charged of all relationships. Nequai and I, realizing that we will always have our differences, are committed to

not letting those differences override our love. And, as in my relationship with my own mother when she was alive, even when we do fuss, we always find our way back to each other.

Most of our feelings of frustration are ego-driven responses to the challenges we face. The ego is that part of us that loves to whine and complain. It learns to be judgmental and demanding, and it always wants to be right. The ego leads us to compare ourselves with others, and when we think we don't measure up, it makes us hide the truth of who we are for fear of being rejected. The ego holds fast to the past, recycling the hurtful experiences we've endured throughout our lives. It coaxes us to dwell on what went wrong in our childhood. But when we are able to retire the ego and look at our lives through the prism of love, we see that no one is perfect and that we develop many of our strengths and sensitivities *because* of our disappointments and hurts. As we relax the ego and put the spirit in charge, we become more forgiving of ourselves and others. We may see how our parents' imperfections, for example, encouraged our inventiveness and taught us how to work around obstacles and take care of ourselves in an imperfect world.

We cannot move our lives forward with the excess baggage of hurt and anger weighing us down. Some of us are still mad at old lovers, former teachers and folks from

the third grade who did us wrong. To this day, my eighty-two-year-old uncle remembers the hurt he felt as a five-year-old child living in Trinidad when his father returned the shiny red bicycle that my grandmother had bought for him. When we have painful memories from hurtful experiences, we may feel justified in holding on to the resentment. But resentment is corrosive. It doesn't affect the person we feel anger toward, it destroys the host.

Anytime we decide to, we can let go of anger and pain. Take quiet, introspective time to think about any negative feelings and old hurts you may be holding on to. Make a list of them. No matter how grievous the act or deep the hurt, write it down. Review the list. Acknowledge that these things are in the past. They happened and there is nothing you can do to change that, but you needn't keep them tethered to your heart. Close your eyes and slow your breathing. Allow your body to relax. Ask yourself if you are ready to be free of the pain you've been carrying, if you are willing to give these burdens to God. If the answer is yes, imagine yourself standing high atop a cliff overlooking the ocean, holding the list of hurts in your hands. See the powerful waves swelling in the distance and breaking beneath you as they crash against the rocks. Surrender to its timeless expanse, its eternal rhythm. It is the womb of all life, the Great Mother's healing embrace. Call the name of each per-

God's love doesn't insist on perfection in you. Why should you insist on perfection in others?

son you want to forgive and whisper to each of them from your heart, *I bless you and release you.* Visualize yourself tearing the list of hurts into small pieces and the wind scattering them over the water. Let the ocean carry them away, cleansing you, absolving you, restoring you. Anytime you begin to feel the weight of those burdens again, remind yourself that they are no longer yours, that you've given them to God. Declare with passion, *I go forth free.*

Eric Butterworth teaches that we are not our emotions. Rather, we *have* emotions that are ours to manage and control. "The healing begins when we realize that all incidents are external," he offers, "and the reactions are our own." We are not our hurts, although we have experienced hurt feelings. Rather than asking why a person would do something so hurtful to *us,* we should ask what in a person's consciousness would make him or her do something so hurtful. During his powerful Sunday sermons at New York City's Lincoln Center, Eric often reminds us that no matter how unkindly someone else behaves, the problem is never ours, but theirs. The pain that causes them to strike out should remind us of our own and invite our understanding. We demand much of others yet are easy on ourselves. We should reverse that attitude so that we are easy on others and demanding of ourselves. An affirmation Eric was taught and uses often is "Father, forgive me for expecting in the human what is found only in the divine." If our happiness depends on how others treat us and respond to us, we are vulnerable every moment. We must always remember that people hurt because they themselves are hurting. People who are limited by their pain can only love us in a limited way.

As hard as it may be for us to accept at times, God sends us the divine right relationships for our growth and gives us the divine right parents for our journey. I held on to much of the pain of my childhood until I began to understand that perception is a fluid line between our blessings and our miseries. What was hurtful can be helpful if we make the conscious decision to grow in wisdom, compassion and love.

Love. We hunger for it, yearn to give it, long to receive it. And it's natural that we do. It is a primal urge. Our visceral desire for love is the life force rising within us, seeking to fulfill itself through us, sustaining and healing humanity as it leaps from heart to heart. We are *called* to love. It is the reason for which we came. We don't have to search for love, we *are* love, created in the image and likeness of the Love that created us. Love is our spiritual inheritance, our eternal, unchanging reality. Love isn't something we must look for, but that which we must allow.

When you commit yourself to living love, you feel at peace with yourself because you are in harmony with the

flow of life. Viewing life from the highest perspective, you feel confident and secure. You realize that no matter how things may appear, you are loved and protected. You know you are one with God, and you bring your peace with you wherever you go. You're not looking *for* love, but for opportunities *to* love.

Loving-kindness is charity that should begin at home. Speak kindly to yourself and about yourself. Don't ignore your shortcomings, but don't dwell on them. See them as what they are: part of your life's work, the areas of yourself you will enjoy cultivating along your journey.

If you hunger for a lover, learn first to become your own. Date yourself, romance yourself, spend the weekend comforting and listening to yourself. Bring flowers, fragrance and soothing music. Forget about the TV, the radio, the phone. When love begins with you, you no longer demand from others the love and sustenance you should give yourself.

When we don't honor ourselves, we feel needy and insecure. We easily settle for relationships that devalue us. Last year I wrote an essay about the young women I'd heard call a local radio station one evening to dedicate love songs to men they *thought* they had love relationships with. One after another these young women pleaded with men not to leave them, to love them, to stop seeing other women and

to call. I was stunned and saddened that so many young sisters were willing to accept and even pursue the abusive behavior they described. I wrote about the need for women to discard the fiction we are taught about needing a partner in order to feel worthy, and about the importance of discovering the power—and the joy—of being alone. We cannot avoid being alone, so we'd better learn to love our own company. We learn our greatest life lessons alone. We discover the truth of who we are alone. We develop our relationship with God alone. We are born alone and we die alone. To have healthy relationships with others, we must first be at home with ourselves. If we don't learn how to be great company for ourselves, we'll settle for spending time with just about anyone. And tolerating bad treatment from bad company turns us bitter and hostile, making it difficult for us to open our hearts when an opportunity for a good relationship comes along.

Keith Smith, the twenty-nine-year-old Minority Affairs Coordinator at Penn State, told me that while women say they want relationships with loving, caring and tender men who treat them with respect, that is not the type of men that many of them choose. "I grew up in a houseful of women," Keith shared, "and I was taught to love and respect them." But he says that he and his friends who treat women well are routinely disregarded, and even rejected, in favor of

the kind of abusive men who are the source of so many women's anger and bitterness. I felt Keith's pain when he said, "I am so sick and tired of serving another man's sentence."

Many years ago, when I was in my mid-twenties, I had a passion for a man named Ron. He was smart, sure of himself, an older man other men in the community looked up to. I just knew I was in love, but to this day I can't tell you why. In retrospect, I see that Ron was distant and a selfish lover. He was the first person I knew who had an answering machine, and one day when I was longing to be with him I gave his machine a workout. I must have left half a dozen messages asking him to call me so that we could get together for dinner that evening. I never did hear from him that day, but the next evening he came to my home and we had a conversation that proved to be a turning point in my life. Ron said he wanted to be honest with me. He said he could see that I was serious about him, that I was the kind of woman who wanted to settle down and have a family and that he would only break my heart. His honesty stunned me. But I felt so grateful for it that I reached over and hugged him and thanked him for being *real*. Ron and I went on to become friends, and there is always great warmth between us when we meet. I will always appreciate him for having the courage and decency to tell me the truth about his feelings, for not crushing my heart. For me, ours was an important relationship because I learned to value myself more and to focus on loving with my heart *and* my head. I saw that for any relationship to work, both partners must want the union. And since that day I have chosen to have relationships with people who demonstrate by their words and deeds that they want to grow with me.

When we become expert at loving and caring for ourselves, we feel healthy, centered and strong. We don't need to escape from our reality through shopping, eating, drinking, drugging or losing ourselves in abusive relationships. We feel warm and safe within ourselves. We learn to value everything about ourselves—our bodies and minds, our feelings and needs, our potential, strengths and weaknesses —throughout all the seasons of our lives. We feel free to acknowledge the truth of who we are, realizing that God didn't send us here perfect, but to work *toward* perfection. When we trust fully, accepting ourselves not as we wish to be but as we are, we develop a sense of wholeness that brings us joy. We stop hiding and worrying about whether anyone else sees our flaws. We aren't defensive or judgmental. We know who we are, we know where we stand, and we accept that we—like everyone else in the world—have some growing to do.

One of the greatest lessons I've learned is that people

can only be who they are. They can only interact with us at their level of personal growth and spiritual development. For us to expect the people in our world to be other than who they are is unfair to them and an exercise in frustration for us. The brilliant Nobel Prize–winning writer Toni Morrison said it well when she revealed that she's very tolerant in relationships—not because she's wonderfully generous, but because she has learned to take people as they come. "Their little habits may be aggravating or annoying, but I'm not bothered by that," she explained. "I have something else to do and something else going on inside of me. And assuming that they don't just chip away constantly at my well-being, most people are really interesting. Why should I try to change them?" she chuckled. "They're better than characters in my books." She went on to express the view that we need to commit ourselves to working at relationships with the same intensity we bring to other important things in our lives.

We must resist the tendency to take our lovers for granted. We often speak to those who are closest to us—especially our partners and our children—in ways we would never speak to our coworkers or friends. But we should be more careful, not less, with those we are closest to. Often our greatest lessons evolve from our deepest, most complex relationships.

I've found that you can say and ask for anything if you do it gently and with kind, loving words. Khephra and I are best friends. Entering our seventh year of marriage, we get along like newlyweds—until we get in the car. Then the battle begins. I think he drives too fast. He says I'm a backseat driver and a nag. I'm learning how to help keep the peace between us: "Sweetie" is the magic word. When he's driving faster than I feel is safe and I turn to him with a smile in my voice and simply say, "Sweetie, please slow down a bit. I want us to be together for the next forty years," he slows down and we continue to chat and laugh and love along the way. But when I grip the dashboard and demand through clenched teeth that he stop driving so fast, he responds in kind, and the joy of the journey is gone.

I learned in my first marriage that harsh words can do indelible damage—no matter how much you apologize, you can't take them back. Now I try to communicate in ways that will help keep the love between Khephra and me strong.

I'm trying to complain less and let go of the many unimportant things that can be irritating in relationships, while challenging myself to find loving ways to discuss those things that really matter. I want to speak gently to those I love, the way I'd like them to speak to me. We don't

have to like everything about others to love them. We don't even like everything about ourselves.

I'm married to the best man I know, and I regularly tell him so. Thanking him for his unwavering support, for being a thoughtful, kind and gentle spirit, makes his heart swell with appreciation and love. We must make it a habit to tell our loving partners each day that they are greatly cherished and loved.

Risk loving, and everything you need is yours. Wisdom comes whenever you open your heart. Your purpose in life is made clear, your divine right lover appears, you see that everything you need to sustain yourself is available to you, and all that you give is replenished sevenfold. Generosity of spirit costs nothing and pays a lifetime of dividends. A compliment, a smile, a kind word and tolerance of others are expressions of love everyone can offer. Forgiveness is an act of love each one of us must practice. Love is a way of seeing and a way of being that honors God in everyone we meet. And it changes us in the most fundamental way. All we need to do is welcome the challenge of our relationships, training our eyes to look beyond human behavior to the Presence within. When we seek to live love, we discover through our interactions with others the divinity within ourselves.

The miracle of life is its constant process of renewal. Everything that lives dies, only to be replaced by new life. Our own bodies are a microcosm of this wondrous process. Over the course of a single year, every cell in every organ is replaced. We are always under renovation, always in the process of making repairs. And despite the intervention and assistance of modern medicine, the best explanation for most healing is that the body somehow does it on its own. "A super intelligence exists in each of us which is infinitely

smarter and possessed of technical know-how far beyond our present understanding," explains the renowned biologist Lewis Thomas in his 1979 treasury of essays *The Medusa and the Snail*. The body may grow frail due to illness and aging, but the life force that is our essence is never diminished. Even when we are unaware of it, the creative power and healing consciousness that we call God exist within us.

Our bodies spontaneously coordinate a multitude of functions, maintain perfect harmony in our various systems, and are marvelously self-correcting when any of those systems swings out of balance. As Thomas asserts in his award-winning volume *The Lives of a Cell*, "It is a distortion, with something profoundly disloyal about it, to picture the human being as a teetering, fallible contraption, always needing watching and patching, always on the verge of flapping to pieces. . . . We ought to be developing a much better system for general education about human health, with more curricular time for acknowledgment, and even celebration, of the absolute marvel of good health that is the real lot of most of us, most of the time."

Unfortunately, our conscious selves are much less adept than our bodies at achieving "cures." Too often, in the name of healing, we simply reach for medications to mask or eliminate the symptoms of physical disorder. Instead we

should look deeper within ourselves to try to discover the real message our body is sending us.

Discomfort of any sort is one of the means by which God focuses our attention. Too often it is the only message we will heed. Physical pain has helped many of us learn the life lessons we weren't receptive to when they were offered to us in less dramatic ways. For years I knew I needed to simplify my diet. There had been warning signs all along— an occasional dull pain in my abdomen, indigestion. But I ignored the symptoms until the problem worsened. Eventually I would get a sharp pain in my stomach whenever I ate chicken or beef. The pain got my attention, and I began listening to my body. I went on a guided three-day cleansing fast that helped me break my lifelong pattern of eating poultry and beef. I eliminated them from my diet ten years ago and haven't had those stomach pains since.

Recently, while walking through the aisles of one of the discount megadrugstores that have sprung up all across the country, I was struck by the astonishing number of products that promise to restore failed health: remedies for headache, constipation, gas, indigestion, hemorrhoids, insomnia, nervousness, arthritis, athlete's foot and more. Our poor health is big business and in no small way fuels the economy. Everywhere we turn there is a pitch for products

created to play the role of surrogate doctor, cure-alls designed to dull the pain of our abuse of our bodies.

Good health. It is the most natural thing in the world, an expression of the perfection we mostly take for granted. And how blessed we are that we can take it for granted. Just imagine the overwhelming task we would have if we consciously had to mind the store—if we had to think about breathing, if we had to marshal our white blood cells and plan their strategies of defense against infection, if we had to release various hormones and attend to a thousand other complex functions. If we had to actively cause our own hearts to beat, we could never go to sleep and would probably die of exhaustion. Life as we know it would not, could not, exist. Ironically, we pay most attention to our health when it's less than perfect. Sometimes our body must be in distress before we give it any thought at all. Then the most important thing in the world becomes for us simply to feel good again.

While we should immediately seek effective medical treatment for any serious ailment, we must also become partners with health professionals in our own care. There is much we can learn from an illness if we listen to our body, interpret the ways in which it speaks to us and trust what it tells us. Illness is often a call to be more attentive to our needs and our feelings. I believe it is always a signal for us

Good health is natural, an expression of God's perfection in us.

to look more deeply within ourselves for a lesson we need to learn.

Just after I gave birth to my daughter, I became ill with a kidney infection. To this day, I remember it as the worst pain I've ever experienced. Moving an inch in any direction was excruciating, and I could do nothing except lie still in my bed. But as it turned out, lying still was exactly the remedy I needed. I was at a crossroads in my life. I was faced with making some hard decisions about my marriage and my future. Quiet time, time for reflection, was what I needed most. I would never have taken it, however, given my many responsibilities as a new mother, if I hadn't become ill. When we don't recognize our need for reflection, rest and renewal, God lays the body down.

The language of the body is clear and specific. It speaks to us in ways that help us maintain balance. When we need greater nourishment on any level—spiritual, emotional, mental or physical—the body lets us know. The questions we must ask ourselves when our body is out of tune are: *In what ways must I learn to love myself more? What must I do to regain and maintain my health and strength? How must I change my perspective on life?*

Unhealthy thoughts and emotions are often at the root of illness. Frequently the maladies we find ourselves battling are physical manifestations of our negative attitudes, suppressed emotions, bitterness and fear. Even the medical community, which until recently for the most part rejected the mind-body connection, now recognizes and accepts the powerful link between them.

Many of our foreparents intuitively understood this holistic approach to health. In *The Healing Drum*, Yaya Diallo asserts that harmony is the key to maintaining both personal and communal health. Among the Minianka of his native Mali, where the musicians also act as healers, dance is a form of preventive therapy for the community. It is both a great harmonizing agent and a diagnostic tool, revealing not only the poise and balance but also the arrogance, aggression and more serious mental disturbances of the villagers. Everything about a person shows up in her or his dancing. Once detected, these psychic disturbances can be addressed and the individual and community returned to wholeness.

Many spiritual practitioners believe that sickness and health have their origin in corresponding mental and emotional states. They teach that the negative thought patterns we adopt can cause illness, and that love, the divine flow within us, is the cure. In the classic work *Your Mind Can Heal You*, written by Frederick Bailes in the early 1940's, the author states that we are the "offspring of God" and that our creativity is "limited only by [our] ability to understand this

relationship." He affirms that if we could understand and accept the fact that each of us is a tiny triangle "having identically the same three sides that God the Great Triangle has—the deciding, the creating, and the resulting sides"—then we could change our personal world "as people grasping this marvelous truth are now doing."

Before the discovery of insulin, Bailes healed himself of what he'd been told was incurable diabetes. He said it was the pioneering book by Thomas Troward, *The Creative Process of the Individual*, that introduced him to the concept that the mind has the power to heal the body.

Bailes admitted that his recovery wasn't immediate and that at the time no one he knew believed in Troward's revolutionary idea. "It took some years to come to the point of complete surrender to the flow of Mind," he wrote, "not because I was consciously obstructing, but because the thought was so foreign to what I had been trained to believe that I missed the point repeatedly. Yet there must have been some glimmer of truth in everything I did because there was some improvement right from the start. Laboratory analysis was used to check the results week by week." Bailes went on to encourage readers who were doing their "healing treatment" work to avoid the company of people who constantly speak about illness and to "deliberately see perfection in others whether their deformity is of the body or of the char-

acter." He advised that for healing to take place we must consciously cultivate the spirit of love for those who are different from us, or who differ with us. "Nothing," Bailes offered, "kills the healing consciousness so easily as the habit of criticism." According to Bailes, criticism is equal to hate. "Criticism poisons," he said, "but love heals." We intuitively understand the truth of these words.

Illness is a challenge and, as with any challenge, it signals the need for growth and change. It is a call to be true to ourselves, to respect our needs, to identify whatever is undermining our happiness and clear it out of the way. Illness is often the way in which life teaches us to take charge of ourselves and shows us that we are neither powerless nor helpless.

Angela Passidomo Trafford, a breast-cancer survivor and author of *The Heroic Path: One Woman's Journey from Cancer to Self-Healing*, found that "illness has a voice." She told me recently that learning to listen to that voice within taught her lessons that ultimately saved her life.

In her book, she writes:

> *Cancer was the best thing that ever happened to me. It totally changed my life. . . . I allowed it to totally change my life. I allowed it to enter my life like the spirit of truth and crack me down, crack down my resistance to change—my hardened,*

Our body speaks to us in ways that help us maintain balance; its language is clear and specific.

unforgiving ways, the fear that ruled my actions and thoughts, the hopelessness and negativity that ruled my being and, worst of all, my determination to have my own way and be proven right, even though the tragedy and pain of my existence showed otherwise.

Angela says the book *Love, Medicine and Miracles* by the noted physician Dr. Bernie S. Siegel helped her cure herself of cancer after a second bout with the deadly disease. For three painful years Angela had been embroiled in a custody battle with her ex-husband, who had kidnapped her children from her home in Naples, Florida, and taken them back to the family's former home in New Brunswick, Canada. Angela says she felt so beaten down from years in an abusive marriage that she couldn't even effectively defend herself when her former husband told the court that it was she who had absconded with the children.

One morning later on, within a ten-minute period, Angela received two devastating phone calls that changed her life. The first was notification that she had lost custody of her three little boys; the second was from her doctor, who told her that tests revealed a recurrence of her breast cancer, which had earlier been arrested by a lumpectomy and eight months of chemotherapy and radiation treatments. "It was a turning point in my life," Angela now realizes. "I was in so

much pain that I couldn't stand to be inside my own body, but there was literally nowhere else for me to turn. I got down on my knees in the middle of my living room, and I don't know where the words came from, but I asked God to forgive me, to take over my life and show me how to live. I really believe that that day I connected with an energy I call the living reality of God."

Afterward Angela, in a haze of fear, got into her car and drove aimlessly around town, somehow ending up at the local public library. That Angela was hurting was obvious. A librarian whom she had never met came up to her and put a book in her hand. It was the book by Bernie Siegel.

Bernie Siegel's story is well known. After becoming despondent about the many people dying of cancer, the former surgeon experienced a spiritual awakening and gave up practicing traditional medicine. Siegel, who has been called "a revolutionary hero of the medical profession," authored two best-selling books on the healing power of love; he has dedicated his life to teaching cancer patients how to heal themselves through self-love, visualization and meditation.

"I took the book home, sat in my armchair and cried as I read it," Angela recalls. "It was a book about taking responsibility for our happiness, wholeness and health." Angela says that despite the pain and depression she was feel-

ing, she decided that she wanted to live. "Never before had I understood that the gift of life is an extraordinarily miraculous fact in and of itself. I realized also that I had never wanted to embrace life for myself—it had always been for someone else."

In the three weeks before her scheduled surgery, she embarked on a spiritual journey that would transform her life. "I was broken down to a state of complete humility. I turned to God, and God told me to be a child again." Angela says she began getting up at dawn each morning to watch the first pink rays of sunlight sweeping the sky. She gave thanks for her life throughout the day and felt for the first time a rush of energy that she now describes as the healing energy of hope. After her daily bike ride, Angela would return home and sit in front of her aquarium doing meditation and visualization exercises using Bernie Siegel's *Love, Medicine and Miracles* as her guide.

"To my amazement," Angela says, "a visualization came forth from within myself of little birds eating golden crumbs; the little birds were the immune-system cells, and the golden crumbs the cancer cells. I would follow this visualization by imagining a white light coming through the top of my head, flowing through my body, healing me." Angela later realized that the visualization of little birds eating golden crumbs was related to a recurring dream she'd been

having of being locked out of a bakery with all the treats inside. "As a child my father would often take me to a bakery. I recognized that that was where the golden crumbs came from and that I was feeding myself the love that I needed but never received from my father," she says. Angela continued to ride her bike and do her meditation and visualization exercises. One day during her "golden crumbs" ritual, she experienced the white light flowing through her body with tremendous energy and force. The heat and intensity of it frightened her, but she recognized her fear as no more than a relentless tape that was replaying the apprehension and mistrust her rational mind had recorded over a lifetime. The moment she let go of the fear and gave herself up to trusting God "was the moment I experienced heaven, and I knew that my healing had occurred."

"The next week," Angela continues, "I was due for my appointment with the doctor. He wanted to discuss the course of treatment and get a closer look at the cancer. After I had the mammogram, the technician said I had to undress again because the doctor wanted me to have another one." This happened eight times that day, and when the doctor finally came in to see Angela, he told her what she already knew: *The cancer had disappeared.* When Angela described her healing experience to him, the doctor said, "Call it what you will. All I know is that you are a very lucky

Healing occurs as you allow the spirit of love to flow within you.

woman." Angela says that Bernie Siegel saved her life by showing her how to use "the gift of cancer" as a vehicle for change. "It was a miracle," Angela says with great joy. "I had a spontaneous healing of cancer. I cannot express the boundless gratitude I feel."

Today Angela Passidomo Trafford is healthy and strong and helping to transform lives through her spiritual healing practice, Self-Healing, in her town of Naples. Three and a half years ago she got her sons back, and she says she now understands why she had to give them up for a time: "I had to be alone. When other people were in my life, I would give my power away. But once you learn to make choices based on self-esteem, you create a wonderful life."

Several years ago Angela invited Bernie Siegel to do a lecture on healing for the Naples community. "Now Bernie and I do workshops together," she says. "He taught me that opening to love is a choice we make, and that's where the healing lies. I could have chosen not to have the healing and to listen to the fear. But love is such a powerful force; it can heal your life, your relationships and your body. First you must find it within yourself."

If we have a health challenge, we can ask God what we are to learn from the illness. Ask for help to locate the life-spring of love that lies at our core. We can learn to draw from that reservoir of love, rather than giving in to the habit

of anxiety. We can determine what is causing us stress so that we can work to get rid of our stressors. Symptoms are an outer expression of illness. If you commit yourself to doing your healing inner work daily, you will dissolve any mental or emotional cause. Find a way to lighten the load. Let yourself marvel at the natural wonder all around you: the new promise of the early-morning sky, the dew on leaves, the newness of each season. Get up early. Meditate. Throughout the day give thanks for your life. Put a smile in your heart, knowing that renewal is *always* possible. Hold fast to your hope, and remember that a positive mental attitude and depression-free states of mind are tremendously helpful in ridding the body of illness and the pain that accompanies disease or injury.

It is up to each of us to take charge of our health. Listen to your body; devote yourself to learning what it must have to stay healthy. Seek out the best and most highly trained and sensitive doctors you can find. As Eric Butterworth says, "Beyond illness there is an 'allness' " that is our natural state of wholeness, one we can return to by opening our consciousness and changing our habits. This state of wholeness—of mental, physical and spiritual unity—begins with each of us as individuals and, through our well-being and enlightenment, extends to all life.

Transition

When Mommy died, I thought I'd never stop crying, never breathe easily again. I ached to my very core. For the first time I understood the profound sense of loss my dear friend Pat Ramsay had expressed when her mother passed away the previous year. I had flown to Jamaica to be with Pat, and as we clung to each other among the thousands of happy travelers moving around us at Norman Manley Airport, she spoke of what now seemed such inadequate expressions of sympathy—the card, the hug, the pat on the back—she had offered to friends who'd lost their mother. Until she lost her own, she confided, she'd had no sense of the depth of sorrow and utter despair they must have been feeling. "I feel so alone," she sobbed. "Now I have no one to pray for me, to intercede for me, no one between me and God."

Neither of our parents died prematurely, out of season. Both were in their early eighties and had lived long and fruitful lives. No matter how old or ill our parents are, we don't want them to leave; yet it's a fact of life that when the spirit is ready to return home to Spirit, it takes flight, whether the body is nine or ninety.

All spirits that travel the earth return to nourish the great Mother Spirit, just as all matter returns to nourish the earth. Nature has much to teach us about life and death. The dead and decaying leaves and fruits of seasons past and the earthly remains of all life fertilize the earth, encouraging new growth, feeding new life in a complete and unending cycle. Our very breath fuels the process: As we inhale, our lungs extract oxygen from the air and expel the carbon dioxide that feeds the plants and trees. Plants absorb our carbon dioxide and release the oxygen we need back into the air, completing another perfect cycle.

Scientists know that neither energy nor matter is created or destroyed, only transformed from one state into the other. What *is* always was and always will be, including

every atom, every spark of energy we are made of. There is
no loss in the universe. My mother's growing dependence
and eventual transition taught me that truth. And although
my beloved Babs's death was staggeringly painful, it has
given me the gift of a richer, more meaningful life.

The period prior to my mother's transition brought
many gifts along with the pain. During the nine months she
lay ailing, I was able to hug and hold her the way I'd always
wanted her to embrace me. I was able to nurture her, to ca-
ress her and tell her how much I cherished her. Moms was
not at all demonstrative and would never have permitted
that show of love and tenderness had she been alert and
strong. Like my father (who had made his own transition
twenty years earlier, when I was just out of my teens), she
was uncomfortable with displays of affection. She had been
a housewife all her life; her days had revolved around her
family. She took perfect care of her children, but always
seemed to me distant and sad.

By the time my mother's health began to slip, I had
come to terms with not having the warm and intimate relationship with her I'd hungered for since I was a little girl.
My healing had begun years before when, as she aged, she
more willingly shared some of her most private truths. I
urged Babs to talk to me about her life, about the secret
hurts and unrealized dreams that so many women of her

generation have tucked quietly away, but have not forgotten. I discovered that beneath my mother's stoic demeanor lay a heart that had yearned for a fuller life—she'd longed to work outside the home, to have her own money, to travel, to have free-roaming conversation with women friends and a greater involvement with the world. But my Trinidadian mother had married a reclusive man.

My father was born in 1898 on the sleepy little Caribbean island of St. Kitts, worlds away from the social clamor of Harlem. Lawrence was a quiet, stern and fiercely private man. He'd married late in life, was a good provider for his family, but was emotionally closed. When I was growing up, no friend of his ever visited our household— except for Mrs. Gibbs, with whom he played the numbers each weekday morning. No friends of my parents ever came to dinner. I'd always thought that was also my mother's choice, but so many years later, when she shared her recollections with me, I learned that she had felt as stifled as I had at times in the quiet and isolated atmosphere of our home. As I grew in understanding of what had depressed and silenced my mother, I was freed from taking her coolness personally. I also began to see that too often we demand perfection of our mothers, insisting that they love us in exactly the way we want to be loved, and wanting them to accept our love in exactly the way we want to give it.

Daughters often put more weight on their mothers' shoulders than anyone should have to bear.

After a second stroke, my mother lost most of her mobility. At first I felt guilty for not bringing her back to the family home. I'd been making plans to do so when, during a meeting with the social worker at the rehabilitation institute where Babs had spent several months in therapy, I had to reconsider. We were going over the renovations that would have to be made to accommodate Mommy's wheelchair when the social worker realized that, given the configuration of the brownstone building, in the event of a fire my mother would be trapped. I was digesting this discouraging new information when my sister, Lillian, and my daughter, Nequai, each of whom have apartments in the building, put their arms around me and asked that I step out of the office. They reminded me of the many arduous days at home after my mother's first major stroke, days when her caregivers were late or didn't show up at all. They pointed out that Moms was still mentally alert then and through therapy had regained the ability to walk. The situation was different now. Although her devoted physician, Dr. Cordia Beverley, had worked passionately and aggressively to rehabilitate her, my mother remained confined to a wheelchair, her mind lost in the past.

Over the years, whenever I'd taken her to visit her ag-

ing friends in nursing homes, I'd promised myself that my mother would never end up in such a place—that she would always be cared for at home. Now I was forced to learn a difficult lesson: Never say never.

Although our hearts were breaking, my brother, Larry, Lillian and I quickly set about finding the best nursing home for our mother. After interviewing knowledgeable health-care workers and friends who had faced similar challenges, and after making visits to several sites, we decided on a small nursing home just a mile north of my apartment. We were grateful to learn that Babs would share a large airy room with three other women. Her bed would be next to a window that looked out on Riverside Park and the Hudson River. *God is so good,* I was reminded throughout this sad and challenging time. Once again I could see clearly how the Creator works through us. When we make a decision and try our best to do the right thing and keep moving forward, Spirit opens the way. Everything needed for Babs to get settled into her new home had fallen smoothly into place.

My mother had herself assisted the process. In the years before she became ill, when her body was still healthy and her mind strong, Babs would periodically call us to sit with her and review her personal papers. Invariably we'd resist, insisting that she'd be around for a long time to come. But she would tell us that we were being foolish. "I've got to

die sometime," she'd declare, "and I don't want any confusion or 'com-mess' [one of her favorite Trinidadian expressions, meaning "an utter mess"] when I'm gone. Now come, sit yourselves down and let me tell you what's what." Wisely, my mother had recognized the inevitable; she had made peace with the one thing that her children couldn't bear to admit—that she would one day make her transition. So when the time came for us to take her affairs in hand, we knew just where every document was located and precisely what we needed to do.

Thank God for my mother's foresight. A second stroke weakened her body and her will. It was then that Mommy started traveling back in time and, for the first time in my recollection, seemed truly happy and at ease. Each time I visited her, she greeted me with loving, smiling eyes and outstretched arms. I was like a sponge. I wanted to be with my mother every possible moment, to absorb her new openheartedness.

Sadly, two months after her arrival at the nursing home, Moms had a devastating seizure that left her bedridden and unable to talk. The nursing-home doctors told me there was nothing more they could do for her and that she could pass away any day. As I stood there at her bedside, I thought: *There lies the woman who put her life, her happiness, on hold for me.* Babs had made the ultimate sacrifice, one I wouldn't

have made. She'd stayed in a confining marriage so that she could raise her children without disrupting our lives. I'd seen Mommy put cardboard in her worn-out shoes so that we could have new ones. She had converted to Catholicism and pinched money from the cash register in Daddy's clothing store to give us the best education available in our Harlem neighborhood—at the local Catholic school. Now, watching her lying in bed, defenseless and unresponsive, I refused to accept the finality of the doctor's words. I refused to give up hope. I was determined to prolong my mother's life and to make her as comfortable as possible.

In the months that followed, I learned many lessons about bringing comfort to our loved ones and helping them make a smooth transition. In the past, when I'd visited my mother or friends in the hospital, I had sometimes accused the nurses and aides of being curt and insensitive. Now that I was spending hours each day at the nursing home, I could see that the workers were overwhelmed. They had too much to do and too few hands to do it. But I discovered, during the months Babs traveled back and forth between the nursing home and the hospital, that when patient care is less than excellent, it improves when it becomes evident loved ones are involved and monitoring the patient's care.

You might be surprised at the extent to which some hospitals and nursing homes will allow you to participate in

the care of an ailing family member, as long as you have a sound plan and discuss it with the person in charge. Babs had become immobile and incontinent. I didn't want her to get bedsores or a rash from soiled diapers, so I requested that the staff change and turn her from side to side more frequently throughout the day. If I thought someone wasn't handling my mother gently, I would pause and ask that person kindly to "Please treat my beloved with the same reverence with which you would want me to treat yours."

At first the nursing staff resisted my efforts to help them with my mother, but in time they accepted me as a partner in her care. I kept my own stock of surgical gloves, wipes and creams at her bedside and learned how to wash her and change her gown and the bed linens, how to turn her and exercise her limbs. During this time I often recalled the riddle of the Sphinx, which my mother quoted frequently as she grew older and felt the frustration of her memory and agility beginning to fail: "Once a man, twice a child." It was now true: Babs had become my baby.

Every experience serves to focus us on the meaning of life, and nothing does that more than facing our own mortality or the imminent passing of a loved one. Although I wasn't aware of it at the time, while I was caring for my mother, I was learning an important life ritual that isn't taught in our youth-oriented society. By performing the rit-

ual of helping my mother through her transition, I was giving a new dimension to my life. I was unconsciously evoking and celebrating the spiritual connection that exists between mothers and daughters. In retrospect, the ritual I was practicing felt like the most loving and natural thing to do, a variation on the rituals our foremothers had adopted to assist their loved ones in making their transition centuries before. I saw my place in the continuum.

Lillian brought our mother's rosary beads and cherished picture of Jesus from home and hung them on the wall near her bed. We placed our family portrait on her nightstand. Although she seemed to have lost her vision by then, the photograph symbolized the fruits of her life's labor and reminded the hospital staff that she was part of a loving family. A glass of clear water, the elixir of life, was always at her bedside. We kept fresh flowers on the windowsill and placed a small tape player near her so that she could listen to her favorite music throughout the day. Babs particularly loved the sweet sounds of Nat King Cole and the soothing spirituals recorded by Jessye Norman and Kathleen Battle.

During this period I reached out to a network of holistic healers in Manhattan: Daya, Dr. Ronald Davidson and Dr. Jifunza Wright. Any advice they offered that felt intuitively right to me became part of the ritual. The nursing

home agreed to let us take Mommy off the liquid food supplement they'd been feeding her through a tube and replace it with a mixture of Chinese herbs, spirulina (a protein-and-nutrient-rich algae) and fresh vegetable and fruit juices. Babs responded well and for a short time even began eating solid food again.

Healer Asar Ha-Pi, who lives in Chicago and teaches an ancient form of Egyptian yoga, shared some massage techniques he had used to comfort his father through his transition. He suggested I massage my mother's temples and feet with olive oil each day. This became my cherished daily ritual. I enjoyed the feeling of intimacy and closeness that arose from being able to comfort her. I extended my massages to include her face, neck, arms and legs, and I whispered her favorite prayers to her during this treasured time. It gave me great pleasure to dab soothing and familiar fragrances under Mommy's nose. I knew that lavender, gardenia and bay rum—the fresh, spicy scent that many older Caribbean people are so fond of—would please her.

Much to the doctors' amazement, Babs was still clinging to life months after they thought she would have died. When Pat Ramsay, who is a former nurse, came from Jamaica for a visit, she helped me to see that my mother was suffering, and possibly holding on to life for me. Pat suggested that I release my mother and tell her it was all right

to leave. As Moms had often said, death is not a punishment, but a resting place for the weary.

A week after Pat returned to Jamaica, I did just that. I whispered to my mother that I now felt capable and strong, that I would have her spirit with me always and it was all right to let her physical body go. I draped a piece of kente cloth on top of her covers. The rich, colorful cloth, woven over the centuries by the Ashanti of Ghana, symbolized that a faithful daughter, a queen, was going home. I promised my mother I'd keep the family together and wear the mantle that she and her mother and grands had decorated so brilliantly in their lives.

A few days later, Mommy made her transition. After her spirit left, I prayed over her body, holding her hand. I had never seen such stillness. It had never been more evident to me that life is breath, not flesh. My mother's body lay in the bed, but my beloved Babs had gone home.

Our faith in life rarely extends to faith in passing over to the place we call death. But death, too, is part of God's plan. It is a natural transition from life as we understand it— a passage we all must face, but which our society treats as a great taboo. We are seldom encouraged to accept our mortality, and we're offered little help in dealing with the anguish of losing a loved one. But we would be much less anxious about our own eventual transition, and much more

sensitive and supportive of those we love who are ailing and aged, if our view of life included the inevitability of death.

I will be forever grateful that, unlike so many instances when our loved ones make their transition, I'd had many years to show my mother my gratitude for the sacrifices she'd made for me. I am one of the lucky ones: I had the chance to bid my mother farewell. I meet so many throughout the country who are not so fortunate, whose loved ones have died violently and without warning.

Recently Khephra and I spent an unforgettable morning with mothers whose children had been murdered. We became the honorary cochairs of an effort spearheaded by New York City television producer Andrea Andrews to build the Children's Peace Memorial, a monument similar in vision to the Vietnam Veterans' War Memorial in Washington, D.C. Andrea and the mothers who came together that morning are dedicated to gathering names of children throughout the country who have been murdered. They are determined to focus the nation's attention on the violence being done to our children. Like many grieving parents who have organized throughout the nation, they are determined to stop the flood of guns and drugs that are snuffing out the lives of youngsters everywhere in America.

Frances Davis, a leader of the group, has experienced the pinnacle of pain. I'd met Frances the year before, while

visiting KidSpeak, a support program that helps young first-time offenders get their lives back on track.

Over a six-year period, all three of Frances Davis's sons had been gunned down in the streets of Brooklyn. Frances had not been present to say good-bye to any of them, and in the months that followed the death of her last son, she cast around in utter anguish until she found a way to give some meaning to her tragedy. When I met her at KidSpeak, she was doing what has become her life's work: talking to our youngsters about the suffering that escalating violence in inner-city neighborhoods is causing families throughout the nation. Frances got their attention.

Her eldest son, Raleak, had been murdered at the age of twenty one night in June 1987 when he and his fiancée were coming out of a grocery store. Raleak had been paid earlier that day; when someone tried to rob him, he resisted. As his fiancée looked on in horror, the robber shot him. Frances told me that Raleak lay bleeding on the sidewalk for twenty minutes before the ambulance came. She recalled her wild-eyed vigil outside the operating room waiting for word of her son's condition: Finally a young female physician, whose face she says she'll never forget, approached and told her, "He didn't make it."

"I couldn't believe it," Frances told me. "I said I had to see him. Raleak lay there dead. My wonderful son, a person

who had so much life, was lying there lifeless. I was just numb." The next day she had to go to the morgue and identify Raleak's body. It was, Frances said, the hardest thing she has ever had to do. "I didn't recognize him," she remembered. "His color was gone. His hair was green, his eyes were gray."

As a child, Frances had been assured that lightning never strikes the same place twice. But she had an eerie sense of foreboding one Saturday afternoon in November 1991. She had taken her youngest child, Frankie, with her on a shopping trip to a discount mall in Pennsylvania. The entire time they were there she was unable to shake the feeling that something was terribly wrong, so they cut the trip short and came back to Brooklyn early. She arrived home to learn that her second son, twenty-two-year-old Andrew, had been shot. He had gotten into a fight on his way to visit his grandmother in the projects. Frances knew that Andrew would never have looked for trouble—especially after his older brother's murder—but he was a big guy, and he wouldn't have backed away from it, either. "They say he won," she says sadly. "He went up to my mother's apartment, and on the way out of the building, the young man he had the fight with wanted to get into it again." When it was over, Andrew lay in the street with four bullets in his body, just a few feet away from his grandmother's building.

"I never got to speak with him again," Frances said.

"Andrew lived for twelve days without regaining consciousness, and on each of those days a little piece of me died." She added quietly, "I buried Andrew with his brother."

Frankie, her remaining son, was then seventeen years old, and an emotionally devastated Frances became focused on one thing alone: keeping him alive. "I didn't want to let him out of my sight," Frances admitted, "but I knew I had to give him a little slack. I felt more sorry for him than myself. He had lost his two older brothers, and not long before Andrew was murdered he'd lost his father too. My husband died in 1989 of an aneurysm. He was thirty-nine, I was thirty-eight."

Frankie wasn't in the least bit streetwise. Everyone called him a mama's boy. Frankie had always wanted to visit Disney World, and by the summer of 1993 Frances had finally saved enough money for them to go. "We were to leave on July 10," she said, "and a few days earlier, he spent the night at my mother's so he could baby-sit the three grandchildren she is raising. She had an appointment early the next morning." Frances hadn't wanted Frankie to leave her mother's house alone, so she had planned to pick him up after she got her hair done.

"I hadn't been in the beauty parlor forty minutes when my sister called and said that I should go to the hospital," Frances remembered. "I couldn't move. I was paralyzed."

The fiancées of her two slain sons came to get her. "Is it Frankie? Is it Frankie?" she kept asking them. "I wouldn't leave the salon until they told me he was alive." Finally they confirmed her greatest fear. "Frankie had left my mother's at noon to come home and start packing for our trip. On the way, he caught a bullet meant for someone else." Frankie was dead.

How could this have happened to her? How could her three sons be gone? All that Frances could think of was burying her last son, then going home and killing herself.

She had lost faith in everything.

"What, I wondered, had I ever done in my life to deserve this? I had always been compassionate. My house was always filled with children. My sons' friends were always welcome at my house. I wasn't a perfect mother, but I was honest with my children. They were my friends. When my husband and I had separated, they were my protectors. My sons were fine young men—they didn't drink or smoke, they weren't involved with drugs—and yet they are gone. And they died in the order in which they were born."

For a long time after Frankie's murder, Frances now says, she was alive but not truly living. She felt as though she didn't belong anywhere. "I didn't know how to pray anymore," she recalls. "I was outraged at God. I would wake up in the middle of the night and scream, 'How could you

do this to me? How could you take my sons?' But even while I was railing at God, a connection was being made."

Hundreds of cards and letters offering solace and support poured in. One card in particular touched her deeply, and she would read it again and again. It included this well-known passage from *The Prophet* by Kahlil Gibran:

> *Your children are not your children.*
> *They are the sons and daughters of Life*
> *longing for itself.*
> *They come through you but not from you,*
> *And though they are with you yet they*
> *belong not to you.*

The pain of losing a loved one is a reminder of how blessed we are to have loved.

"The woman who sent the card wrote that God never gives us more than we can bear," Frances says, "and I began to believe that maybe it was true. After all I'd been through, I was still here." Soon she began to speak to God in a different way. She told God that she no longer knew how to pray with faith, but that she was going to pray anyway. Although she can't pinpoint when it began to happen, she realized one day that she didn't feel angry anymore.

Frances began reading the newspapers again, and saw that she wasn't the only one suffering. "So many young peo-

ple are dying," she says urgently. "Children. Young mothers caught in the crossfire of urban violence. I started praying for guidance and felt that, as hard as it is to speak about my children in the past tense and to tell my story, I could help our young people if I began to speak out."

Today Frances Davis is part of several support groups of parents whose children have been murdered. "Going out and helping others has helped to heal my own heart," she explains. She speaks to youngsters at high schools and to families at workshops on grief and loss. "So many mothers have told me that they felt guilty when their children were killed," says Frances. "I did, too. Although my sons weren't killed in our neighborhood, I felt that I should have moved far away. I had to remind myself often that I was a good mother, and that made me feel a little better." Frances adds that when Black men are murdered, "the media makes you feel that they weren't completely innocent, that in some way they contributed to their own victimization."

No convictions were made in the murders of Raleak or Andrew. The young man who killed Frankie was sentenced to twenty-seven years to life. "I felt sorry for him," Frances admits. "I don't want us to lock up our children and throw away the key. I'm tired of seeing them buried or going to prison, which is another death. Instead I want to see a change in our society." She shares her passionate conviction that we must petition for stricter gun-control laws. "I want to see our children get their lives back," she declares. "The schools aren't working, our children can't find jobs. They are routinely harassed by police. My heart bleeds for our children. I'm tired of hearing them say they feel old when they make it to eighteen and are still alive."

Frances says that the work she is doing now is the work she must do in order to make her children's deaths count for something. "Today I look at death differently," she offers. "That my children are gone is a part of God's plan. I know there is a power higher than me. I don't question it anymore. I have my sadness, but I am able to live with it and still move forward because I have faith and my life has purpose. My whole life was about being a mother. Now I am a mother to any child who needs me. I will do anything within my power to help any child in need. And that commitment has changed my life."

Frances Davis's life today is a powerful reminder that there is no depth of emotional pain from which we cannot recover, and that we can give positive value to our most painful experiences. "I know that people feel sorry for me when they hear my story," Frances admits, "but I came through it, and one of the many lessons this great tragedy has taught me is that every hurt can be healed—if you have faith in God, if only you believe."

As physical manifestations of the Divine, each of us has reserves of strength we can draw on in times of crisis. But until we are tested, we won't fully appreciate this. And that is why we must allow ourselves the time to grieve.

Grief is a natural response to the death of a loved one, and an important part of the healing process. Before the healing can even begin, we have to acknowledge the pain and yield to it. We have to accept the fact of our new reality and express the truth of our feelings about the loss—even if others are uncomfortable with expressions of powerful, painful emotions. When my friend Ronnie Grant lost his mother earlier this year, people told him to be strong and not to cry. "How can I not cry?" Ronnie implored. "I just lost my mother, my best friend of more than forty years."

Unexpressed grief can be destructive. It can make us intensely angry, fearful of intimacy and dependent on substances that dull or mask the pain, which will lead to other emotional problems down the road. We should seek out those with whom we feel comfortable talking about our hurt, as we experience it.

The pain of losing a loved one is also a reminder of how blessed we are to have loved. But if we feel ourselves slipping into a deep depression or have difficulty coping with the loss and moving on with our lives, we should reach out for help. We should join a grief-recovery support group

or talk to a minister or therapist. Above all, we must ask God to heal our hearts.

One of the most helpful things we can do for someone who is grieving is to stay in touch. It often happens that within a week following the funeral, people have forgotten about the bereaved, or have forgotten that the person left behind is still in a lot of pain. Remember to give a friend who is in mourning a call each day. Ask "How are you doing today? What are you feeling?" and allow her or him to tell you, or else to say nothing. We can be of great comfort to grieving hearts simply by lending an ear and allowing those who are bereft to express just how much they hurt.

We can find solace in reminiscing about those whom we have lost, in recounting the stories that best characterize them, in laughing at the humorous moments we have shared. By sharing such stories, we keep our memories of our loved ones alive and remind ourselves of the ways our lives have been touched by theirs. In West Africa it is believed that the deceased continue to live for as long as there is someone to call their names. By allowing a small spark of our loved one's spirit to live on in us, they remain with us still.

Remember, too, that life only *appears* to begin with birth and end with death. The flow of life is in fact continuous and eternal; birth and death are merely transforma-

The flow of life is continuous and eternal; birth and death are merely transformations.

tions. We are made up physically and spiritually of the billions who have passed before us. They gave us life, they gave us our culture, they gave us the world on which we have built our present world. Our values and traditions, our habits of thought are in large measure the wisdom of their experience passed down through the ages. Our breath, the very air we breathe, was once their breath. We are, each of us, an integral part of something vast beyond comprehension—a vital link in a process so perfect that it wants for nothing and wastes nothing. That something is life. Death, the inevitability of it, or the illusion of it, helps us to think about and appreciate the miracle we are moving through.

Our lives are characterized by transitions and transformations, by necessary losses and unexpected gifts, by an unending series of passages. Life is change. All our lives we are confronted with letting go. Western culture teaches us how to hold on to things, not how to let them go, but letting go is one of the encompassing themes of life. Nothing in the material world is forever. Throughout the many stages of our lives we experience myriad transitions and what we might call loss: We are forced to leave the warmth and security of our mother's womb, give up her breasts, her lap, our innocence, many of our childhood dreams, our youth. Critical to our growth and happiness is learning how to live with loss; we simply cannot have everything as we

143

wish it. Parents, children, lovers and friends part, and sometimes it is we who must leave. Our lives are full of separations that shake us up, force us to attend to our emotional selves and to learn new ways of being in the world. Although many of our losses are painful, they encourage our gains. The lesson life is trying to teach us is that, regardless of the challenges and changes in the physical world, we will abide in peace by aligning ourselves with our inner changelessness. The power of God in us is more than equal to any moment—no matter what it brings. We live in a loving, supportive universe that is always saying yes to us. Every transition, even the one we call death, is part of a continuum of being. Death is not the end, but rather another step in the unending process of our unfolding. It is a pathway to God. It may sometimes seem as if our baptisms are all of fire, but in the fire we forge new strengths. Though we sometimes despair, the wakes we plan for ourselves are always premature. Time and again we emerge from this chrysalis changed, remade, born again. This is the pattern for all life, the end of each journey marking the beginning of new and different ones. Have faith. When those who are dear to us make their transition, when we ourselves approach with trepidation that threshold of infinity, know that their lives and ours are cared for by a power greater than any pain.

What Would You Give?

It is a special blessing to have the gifts of human intelligence and free will, to have the power to think and move and change, the ability to dream and shape the world. We are a remarkable species at an extraordinary time in history, a marvel of God's expression. All the natural resources we need to thrive are available in abundance on this little rock floating in space. We have enough—enough air, enough food, land and fuel, enough water to share. We have the knowledge, skills and technology to solve all our personal and social crises. Everything we need is already present around us—

everything, it seems, except enough common sense, justice and love.

A narrative describing our society today would read like bad fiction: Millions of hungry and homeless people living in the wealthiest country in the world; the most vulnerable in our midst—children and the elderly—suffering the most; troops defending foreign borders while an avalanche of drugs crosses our own; silent workers wringing their hands as their jobs vanish; families deathly afraid of crime, but addicted to watching heinous acts of violence for entertainment. And everyone naming and blaming and pointing the finger at others—at "shiftless Black folks," at "racist White folks," at foreigners they think should go home, at heartless politicians, at inefficient government policies, at greedy, profit-grabbing corporations. It's a sad tale of people who seem to have lost their reverence for life, forgotten their potential and their purpose. But this is not bad fiction, it's the painful truth about our lives. None of the inequities in our society could exist without our complicity. Our society is out of balance because we as individuals are. The pain and suffering all around us are a reflection of our stymied consciousness and of how gravely we are failing to love.

The sad events reported on the evening news confirm our sense that it's the midnight hour, that our worst nightmares have become our waking reality and we should feel

afraid. The paralyzing effect of fear makes us as helpless as babies and blinds us to the truth that God didn't send us here to be powerless spectators, but to become powerful initiators. We are spiritual beings having an earthly experience, and we have the power to break the cycle of negativity that is fueling a very dangerous world. We can create harmony in our lives and in the world. It's not only possible, it is why we are here.

This is the appointed hour. We can choose and we can change. We can change the values, structures and institutions that deny us our wholeness and dishonor the sanctity and unity of life. We can create a new paradigm for living that establishes balance in our lives. But any paradigm that offers us the comfort and peace we are seeking must be spirit-driven, not market-driven. It must have giving rather than taking at its core, and it must be dedicated to preserving the dignity of life rather than winning at any cost.

The balance and peace we seek for ourselves and our society won't be achieved through mental effort alone. Mind and spirit are meant to travel together, with spirit leading the way. Until we make a conscious commitment to understand and embrace our spiritual nature, we will endure the ache of living without the awareness and guidance of the most essential part of ourselves. Ignorance of the most vital aspect of our being makes us vulnerable and easily con-

147

trolled. So we believe the messages that bombard us daily: *You are not complete as you are; you need something outside yourself to make you whole.* We absorb the myth that life is about image—an image that only the right product can confer—rather than about us, the people, about how we feel and about the quality of our lives. We focus on doing instead of on being, on getting rather than on giving. We think money and adoration offer fulfillment.

If we are fortunate, we eventually discover that image is transitory, as insubstantial as a mirage. My work at *Essence* over the years has introduced me to wealthy and famous people from around the world, and some of them are the most miserable people I've ever met. Their fortune hasn't given them the inner security they crave. The great admiration others have for them doesn't make them feel whole.

I'll never forget the story I read a few years ago in *New York Woman* magazine about Helen Hunt, daughter of the late Texas oil billionaire H. L. Hunt. I had known Helen only as a passionate advocate for homeless women and abandoned children. She had reached out to me on occasion to participate in the many grassroots efforts of her New York Women's Foundation. The magazine feature I read was an intimate portrait of a fascinating humanitarian whose teenage daughters spent their summers not vacationing in Europe or sunning at the beach, but tutoring children in

Harlem. But what struck me most and what I wish never to forget is that Helen Hunt, who has more money than she could ever spend, said she felt blessed for another reason. "There is a myth that if you amass enough wealth, then your life falls into place," she explained, "but having been born with great wealth, I know that's not true. And realizing that myth, you really do start out ahead. . . . It's one of the things I've been so grateful for." While Helen Hunt, who has since moved to New Mexico, has her own priorities in order, some of her siblings' lives seem to be a mess. Indeed, much has been written about the discord and infighting within the Hunt family, which have, unfortunately, torn many of their lives apart.

We know that material things don't offer contentment, but still we buy more—more of the props and gadgets our culture tells us we must have in order to be happy and "happening." Our addiction to consumption distracts us from seeing that we are disconnected from ourselves, from our truth and from one another. Any euphoria we experience from our material gains is fleeting at best. Still we feel anxious about the future. Still we fear that our lives are out of control. Ironically, however, in our anxiety and fear we are at one with most of humanity.

Our disquiet is the result of the choices we are making—what we are doing or not doing. Deep within we

yearn to live in alignment with our spiritual values. We hunger to stand for something more—more love, more justice, more peace. We know that our choices don't correspond with our core values or with the future we want for ourselves and our children. We are all experiencing some level of pain.

But pain has its purpose. It focuses our attention on the choices that are causing us harm. Pain is one of the many ways life speaks to us and encourages us to correct our course. The good news we never see on the nightly news is that we *can* correct the course. We have the power—and the responsibility—to create peace and happiness in our lives and to ease the suffering in our world. This is our greatest need—and our only salvation. Committing ourselves to our personal and collective well-being is the only way to create the love we are seeking. Wherever there is hurt, we can heal. Wherever there is sorrow, we can bring joy. We are healers and teachers, we are "earth angels."

All around us there are people who are doing the important work. One of the most inspiring people I've ever met, Alice Harris, is changing lives in her Watts neighborhood. Alice, who grew up in Gadsden, Alabama, went to jail at twelve, became a mother at thirteen and was homeless and suicidal at fifteen because of the blame and shame she endured being labeled "a bad girl." But it was the kindness

Pain is one of the ways life speaks to us and encourages us to correct our course.

and compassion of the woman whose children she cared for that helped Alice turn her life around.

This kind and spirited woman told young Alice she could do anything she put her mind to. She taught the illiterate teenager to read, helped her pass a cosmetology test and supported her in finding a better job in one of Gadsden's finest beauty salons. "The generosity and compassion that were shown to me are what I'm repaying today," says the woman who is known throughout Watts simply as "Sweet Alice." But any debt she owes has been repaid ten thousand times and more through her organization, Parents of Watts. For more than thirty years, and on a shoestring budget, Sweet Alice has created a stunning number of programs that are saving and securing lives. In the complex of eleven houses owned by Parents of Watts, there are programs for teens and at-risk mothers, a food bank, and housing for twenty-one mentally ill people and twenty-eight men and women who are making the transition from prison back into the community. Her Adopt-a-Bus program employs former inmates who work through the transportation department as a security patrol. Sweet Alice has organized Black, White and Latino teachers from a nearby school to teach parenting skills to adults, Spanish to Black folks, and English to their Spanish-speaking neighbors.

When I last spoke with Sweet Alice, this cherubic

151

woman with a million-dollar smile was brimming with excitement and joy about her most recent project: The Children's Paradise. A mansion built by former inmates on half an acre of donated land in a prime area of Altadena, California, The Children's Paradise is a retreat for the children of Watts. "We take them away from the stresses of the inner city and teach them social skills, life skills and spiritual values," she says. "We are trying to meet their needs *before* they get into trouble." Sweet Alice points out that if someone hadn't offered her a helping hand, she wouldn't be here helping others today. "But," she insists, "I didn't create this magnificent project. I don't know how to create anything that big. God did it!"

There is so much good news that we never hear or read about—stories of people who are doing a mighty work. Nisa'a Ameen-Abdullah, a Denver housewife and mother of two young daughters "and four other children I claim," offers support to youngsters who are missing what her own children have. She named her elegant refurbished home in Denver's Black community "Homework House," and after school she tutors girls from her daughters' grammar school who are having difficulty with their homework. Often the children are living with their grandmothers, teen mothers or someone in a crisis situation who is unable to assist them. "I'm the mom who happens to be home in the daytime, and

the kids just love to come here," Nisa'a says. Her friend, Vicki Harvey, a mother of two sons, is also pitching in. She has begun to give the boys in her community homework support after school. Nisa'a says her vision is to have retirees, and anyone else who is at home during the day or the weekend, give our children some time. "This," she explains, "is simple, doable. When you make something easy, you can be consistent with it."

Another person living love is Father George Clements, the activist Catholic priest from Chicago who became nationally known for initiating the One Church—One Child program, dedicated to finding Black adoptive parents for Black and biracial children. In 1981 he set an example for his Holy Angels parish by becoming the first Catholic priest to adopt a child. Father Clements went on to adopt three more sons.

Now living in Washington, D.C., Father Clements is traveling the country launching a new program called One Church—One Addict. This innovative program trains teams of church members to work together to help recovering addicts maintain drug-free lives. With states closing down treatment centers throughout the country, many drug addicts have nowhere to turn. Father Clements believes they should be able to turn to the church. He feels religious institutions have been in massive denial about social issues,

153

and finds that addicts are pleasantly surprised when churches open their doors and hearts to those whom society has treated like modern-day lepers. Addicts, Father Clements reminds us, are routinely rejected by family, friends, employers and even churches. "Addiction itself is a spiritual disease and needs a spiritual cure," he asserts, "and where better to find it than in our Christian churches, Buddhist and Baha'i temples, Muslim mosques and Jewish synagogues, which are supposed to be repositories of love?"

Everywhere I travel I meet women and men who are working to meet critical social needs through support programs initiated by sororities, fraternities, national organizations and community groups. People are volunteering their time, energy and resources in an effort to help those in need. Many of the extraordinary individuals and the "Programs That Work" we report on monthly in *Essence* are those I've been introduced to during my time on the road. Learning about the work that folks are doing to ease the suffering in their communities focuses us on how very blessed we are and on the great possibilities for change.

Last year I met a man who offers a powerful example of how wealthy and talented people can share their blessings. I was the luncheon speaker at the Wharton School's Twentieth Annual Whitney M. Young, Jr., Memorial Conference in Philadelphia, and I shared a ride with another

W h a t
W o u l d
Y o u   G i v e ?

presenter, Lawrence Schumake, the former executive director of the Black Economic Union, now an economic- and
community-development expert in Kansas City, Kansas.
During our short trip to the train station, I asked him a host
of questions about how he felt we could effectively revital-
ize our blighted inner-city neighborhoods. Schumake spoke
fervently about the need for a comprehensive approach that
gives people a voice in their own development and em-
braces the social, physical and economic aspects of their
lives. Anything less than that, he assured me, would have
little impact.

A few days after our discussion, a package of material
arrived with a letter from James Rouse of Columbia, Maryland, founder of The Enterprise Foundation, stating that
Lawrence Schumake had suggested he get in touch with me
about his Sandtown project in Baltimore. In part, the letter
read:

> *Sandtown is a neighborhood of 10,300 people in 72 square blocks*
> *of largely dilapidated housing—44% underemployed, 40%*
> *school dropouts, 50% with incomes under $10,000 a year, the*
> *center of drugs and violent crime in Baltimore.*
>
> *Working with the mayor and with the residents of the*
> *neighborhood, Sandtown is being transformed into a neighborhood*
> *where there is fit and affordable housing for all people, where*
> *children are educated and leave high school ready for work or*

college, with primary health care available to every man, woman and child, with skill training and job placement and support for new small business development.

It is the purpose of the program to demonstrate that the living conditions and the lives of people living at the bottom in the American city can be transformed so that all people can lead productive lives and participate fully in their community.

James Rouse's letter went on to say that he would call my office to see if I was interested in meeting him during a trip he would soon be making to New York City. Yes, I was interested—very much interested in meeting a person who was creating a model for what must be done throughout the world. *James Rouse*, I remember thinking, *seems as if I've heard that name before.* But I didn't make an immediate connection. Then, a few days before our meeting, as I pored over the additional information I had asked his office to send, I was shocked at what I discovered.

This James Rouse was one of the world's largest builders of shopping malls. He had revitalized American cities by creating downtown marketplaces and turning dilapidated harbors into highly profitable enterprise zones. I learned from a *Forbes* magazine cover story on the richest people in America that Jim Rouse had been orphaned at sixteen, had worked his way through law school at night and had gone

We have the power—and the responsibility—to create peace and happiness in our lives and to ease the suffering in our world.

W h a t
W o u l d
Y o u G i v e ?

on to build a great fortune through The Rouse Company, an organization that grew out of the mortgage banking business he'd started in 1939. He had pioneered the enclosed shopping-mall concept in the 1950's, and in the 1960's—before the Civil Rights Act of 1968 barring racial discrimination in housing—he secured 15,000 acres of farmland and built Columbia, Maryland, the first integrated southern community, where he and his wife, Patty, still live along with more than 77,000 other residents. In 1979, at age sixty-five, Jim Rouse left the company he founded to dedicate himself to improving the lives of the poor.

I was excited to meet Jim Rouse for a number of reasons. Here was a man who seemed to understand that the acquisition of wealth, position and power is of little consequence if you lose your soul. Here was an object lesson for an America that had sold its soul again and again. Here was an example of the real American dream, the way America ought to be.

On the day of our meeting, the eighty-year-old master builder arrived, alone, at *Essence*'s Times Square headquarters. He wore a simple sports jacket and walking shoes and carried his own bags. His meeting with us was his last stop before catching a cab to Pennsylvania Station for the train ride back to Maryland. During his visit, he spoke passionately not about the problems, but about the possibilities for solv-

ing urban poverty and giving all people an opportunity to fulfill themselves. "It's not rational that millions of people live in poverty in this affluent society," he declared, "and unless we begin to turn things around, America is going down the chute." Near the end of our visit I asked him why a man with his wealth was spending his golden years on the battlegrounds of inner-city neighborhoods coast-to-coast. "It's a value I hold," Jim Rouse stated simply. "Love thy neighbor as thyself."

It's a lesson we all must learn. But few Americans see themselves in their neighbors when their neighbors don't look like them. Color has blinded us to our common humanity. We aren't one nation, but two, divided, with liberty and justice for some but not all. Before America can become the example of decency that Jim Rouse's life represents, some sort of restitution must be offered for what has never been apologized for or even fully acknowledged. Let the painful truth be told: The very foundation of America was constructed not upon love for one's neighbor, but upon greed, grave injustice and a cruel policy of conquest, slavery and exploitation. Let us not believe that the lack of moral leadership so evident today is a recent thing. It dates back to 1607, when the first English settlers began their brutal conquest of Native Americans in Jamestown, and continued with the expansion of the Atlantic slave trade, which up-

rooted and shattered the lives of more than 100 million Africans. It proceeded with the mid-nineteenth-century policy of Manifest Destiny, which held that European settlers had all rights to whatever lands they chose to claim for America. An apology and economic reparations were made to Japanese-Americans who were interred in relocation camps during World War II, but only after Japan became a powerful economic force. Nothing of this nature has been issued to Native Americans or African-Americans whose ancestors were slaughtered and enslaved by the millions over hundreds of years.

The lessons of the past suggest that racism and resentment against people of color will continue to flourish in America as long as the history that is taught transposes the heroes and the villains. That is the unspoken truth at the heart of the nation's racial divide.

A powerful example of what needs to occur here to begin healing the wounds of racism took place in Ghana on December 6, 1994, during Panafest, the semiannual festival created to bring people of African descent scattered throughout the diaspora back to our homeland. At midnight the tribal leaders representing chiefdoms all over the country assembled in a clearing just outside the capital city of Accra for a ceremony of atonement. They gathered for what is called the "washing of stools and skins," the ancient

Ghanaian ritual of apology. There, shrugging off their red-and-black robes of mourning in a procession and ritual, they asked for forgiveness for their ancestors, those chiefs who centuries ago sold the people from their own villages into slavery. Conniving and greed are an age-old and worldwide sickness. But this sickness can be healed. Visionaries like Sweet Alice Harris, Nisa'a Ameen-Abdullah, Father Clements and James Rouse are part of that healing.

A model for harmonious living won't be created by large corporations. Nor will the government legislate it. And we cannot rely solely on our religious leaders to initiate it. While love is the guiding principle in all the world's major theologies, a religious or spiritual philosophy has no meaning until we practice it and make it a part of our lives. You and I must make the commitment to change our consciousness, to send forth the great surge of love and compassion—and plain common sense—that is sorely needed today. "We are each other's harvest:/we are each other's business:/we are each other's magnitude and bond," writes Gwendolyn Brooks, the wise poet laureate of Illinois. You and I are the leaders, the healers and the teachers we've been waiting for.

More love is our only hope for the future. It is all we need. Without more love, we will keep shifting from one thing to another in a restless search for satisfaction and

peace. But contentment can only be found through self-nur-
turance balanced with service to others. That is when our
joy is full. Fulfillment is not possible without a commitment
to a purpose beyond our own personal existence. By growing in kindness and openheartedness, we satisfy our natural
hunger for love. Love and reciprocity—these are the laws of
creation in which we must put our faith. Whenever we give
of ourselves, we create an ever wider pathway for receiving.
That's the promise: Whatever you give returns to you mul-
tiplied and running over. Our limitless capacity for loving,
for giving and receiving, is the miracle of our existence.

What would you give to make our world a better
place? What would you give to ease the suffering around
you? What do you care deeply about? What will you commit yourself to? Listen inwardly and hear the messages God
sends to your heart. Choose an issue, find a local group
that's working on it and give of yourself as God inspires you
to give. Anyone not actively engaged in easing the suffering
in the world is contributing to the pain.

Be a giving spirit wherever you are. Each day ask God
what you can give, what need you can fill, what information
you can share. There is so much good we can do with little
effort. Put people in touch with the resources they need. Put
those grappling with similar issues in touch with one another. Let's smile more, affirm and encourage the strengths

in others more, rather than criticizing and amplifying weaknesses. Encourage organizations to which you belong to work on social issues. Urge your house of worship to open its doors not just for Saturday and Sunday worship services, but for community-support programs throughout the week.

By organizing around issues and demanding change, we can bring an end to the cycle of poverty and pain that is destroying lives and communities and fueling a very dangerous world. What choice do we really have? We can't build walls high enough or bars strong enough to restrain hungry, hopeless people. The government can't build prisons fast enough to contain those who, for lack of an education or legitimate opportunity, turn to criminal behavior.

As we grow in awareness of our divinity, we gain clarity, think more critically and analyze more keenly. We begin to see how our society too often pits one group against another. We see how the middle class is always charged with paying for whatever little relief is given to the poor, while large corporations and a relatively few individuals amass more and more power and wealth. White males in the work force, fearful of losing their jobs, will see that jobs have been made scarce by greed and an irrational, wasteful system that uses Black people as scapegoats. We'll begin to understand that we're all in the same lifeboat, and that in or-

The more you give, the more you receive; as you heal others, you are healed.

der to survive we must use all our oars to pull smartly in the same direction.

Where we go from here depends on you and me. On how we live our personal lives and on the kindness and compassion we show to one another. By giving love, we tap into the love that is inherent in us. We claim our divinity, opening the way to the higher self. We experience being part of the unity of life, connected with others and with our surroundings.

When you see a need, ask yourself if you can help to fill it. Give yourself to life. Give yourself to love. Love is your secret talisman: The more you give, the more you have to give, and the more you receive. As you help, you are helped. And as you heal others, you yourself are healed.

In our elder years, when we look back on our lives, our joy won't spring from what we gained, but from what we gave. As we reflect on the part we played in helping to reduce the suffering in the world and to create a better place for generations to come, a great peace will fill our hearts. Buoyed by this purest peace, we will be able to move easily from this world to the next, content that our lives had purpose: that we loved, and in loving, learned life's lessons well.